# 3

Rochester College Lectures on Preaching
Volume 3

# *Preaching Romans*

David Fleer and Dave Bland, editors

*Preaching Romans*

# A·C·U
# PRESS

ACU Box 29138
Abilene, TX 79699
www.acu.edu/acupress

Cover Design and Typesetting by Sarah Bales

Printed in the United States of America

ISBN  0-89112-137-4

Library of Congress Card Number:  2002105010

1,2,3,4,5

# Table of Contents

*Biographical Sketches* . . . . . . . . . . . . . . . . . . . *7*

*Foreword* . . . . . . . . . . . . . . . . . . . . . . . . . . . *11*
Paul Scott Wilson

*Introduction* . . . . . . . . . . . . . . . . . . . . . . . *15*
David Fleer and Dave Bland

**Part 1** *Texts, Themes, and Issues in Preaching Romans*

1  *Ethnic Issues, Eschatology, and Moral
   Reasoning in Paul's Letter
   to the Romans* . . . . . . . . . . . . . . . . . . . . . . *24*
   James Walters

2  *Narrative Preaching from Romans* . . . . . *53*
   James Thompson

3  *Paul's Ethic in the Letter to the Romans:
   Preaching that Forms a
   Moral Community* . . . . . . . . . . . . . . . . . . *73*
   Dave Bland

4  *When in Romans: Preaching From the
   Fifth Chapter of Romans* . . . . . . . . . . . . *101*
   Stephen Farris

5  *Funding the Sermon with Gospeled
   Imagination: Reflections on Text and
   Sermon from Romans* . . . . . . . . . . . . . . . *127*
   Mark Love

**Part 2** *Sermons on Romans*

6  *Sermons from Romans 1-8* . . . . . . . . . . *153*
   Mike Cope

7  *Sermons from Romans 9-16* . . . . . . . . . . *199*
   Ken Durham

To the Religion/Theology faculty at Abilene Christian
University (1976-1981), especially professors Tom
Olbricht, John T. Willis, Ian Fair, Everett Ferguson, and
Bill Humble, who taught us a love for the biblical text,
careful scholarship, and a reverence for God.

## Acknowledgements

Special thanks to Josh Fleer, Greg Stevenson, Rick
Oster, Debbie Haskell, Carisse Berryhill, Chris Altrock,
and Jonathan Woodall for close readings of the
manuscript in its various stages of development.

Ministers Mark Frost, Russ Bone, Pete Brazle, Roger
Woods, Mark Brackney, Tom Rellinger, Kent Hoggatt,
and Royce Dickinson provided careful planning for the
2001 Rochester College Sermon Seminar.
We especially acknowledge Curtis McClane for his
enthusiastic dedication to the Seminar and lifelong
commitment to the ministry of preaching.

# Biographical Sketches

## Dave Bland

For more than two decades, Dave Bland has devoted his life to preaching tenures with the Eastside Church of Christ in Portland, Oregon and, currently, with the White Station congregation in Memphis. Dave complements his life's activity in preaching with a background in rhetoric (Ph.D., University of Washington) and has long cultivated an interest in wisdom literature. These experiences have created a thoughtful ministry and serve him well in the chapter in the present volume, which evaluates the preacher's role as moral theologian. In addition to teaching preaching, Dave directs the Doctor of Ministry Program at Harding University Graduate School of Religion.

## Mike Cope

Mike Cope is co-editor of *New Wineskins* magazine and preaches for the Highland Church of Christ in Abilene, Texas. For years, Mike has been a preacher with deep insight into both the human condition and the biblical text. In recent years, before a large college-age audience and out of the compelling story of his own experience, Mike's preaching has been in passionate conversation with Scripture and this world. Preaching, for Mike, can be nurtured even out of the dark places of life.

## *Ken Durham*

Ken Durham preaches for the Malibu Church of Christ in California and is adjunct Professor of Religion and Communication at Pepperdine University. Like Mike Cope, Ken preaches before one of the largest college-age congregations in the Churches of Christ. Cultivating his background in rhetoric (Ph.D., Louisiana State University) with an unwavering affection for Scripture, Ken is noted by his congregations for seriously engaging life's most essential topics through a challenging enactment of the world of Scripture.

## *Stephen Farris*

Stephen Farris is Professor of Preaching and Worship at John Knox College in the Toronto School of Theology. He is book review editor for *Homiletic* and, in 1999, hosted the annual meeting of the Academy of Homiletics. Today he serves as the Academy's President. His article in this volume continues his thesis, developed in *Preaching That Matters* (1998, W/JKP), that analogy can serve as a connecting link from our world to the realities of the Bible. Like his personality, Stephen's writing is thoughtful, kind, and stimulating. He seeks in preaching an encounter with God at the meeting of text and listeners.

## *David Fleer*

David's devotion to preaching first found expression through a long-tenured pulpit ministry with the Vancouver Church of Christ in the state of Washington. His Ph.D. in Speech Communication at the University of Washington moved him into teaching, where he is currently Professor of Religion and Communication at

Rochester College. Co-editor of the current series on preaching, David's work is characterized as a thoughtful and passionate attempt to walk afresh in the world of Scripture that readers and listeners may experience the reality of the Gospel of God.

## *Mark Love*

Mark Love is Assistant Professor of Bible and Ministry in the Graduate School of Theology and Director of Ministry Events at Abilene Christian University. He has just completed an eleven-year tenure as Minister of the Word with the East County Church of Christ in Gresham, Oregon. The foundation of Mark's work in congregational ministry and teaching is that theology matters. Theological reflection is the source of Mark's creativity and robust devotion to the art of preaching. Mark's article in this volume appropriately expresses his conviction that the Gospel should impact both the form and content of our preaching.

## *James Thompson*

James Thompson's training and practice is in New Testament studies, with specific interest in Pauline literature. From this foundation, James has integrated an interest in preaching as a practical expression of his textual work. He is a founder of the sermon seminars now held across the country, Professor of New Testament at Abilene Christian University, editor of *Restoration Quarterly,* and author of *Preaching Like Paul* (2000, W/JKP). In each aspect of his work, James reminds us of our better instincts, that the Bible reveals the source of our hope, the good news found in Jesus Christ.

## *James Walters*

James Walters is known for his ability to communicate with clarity the thinking of Paul and other New Testament writers. James' feet are planted in two radically different worlds. In one world, James does research in archeology and textual studies, is Professor of Theology at Boston University, and provides leadership in the Society for Biblical Literature. James' other world is revealed in his work with Heartbeat Urban Initiatives Program, whose task is to communicate the message of Christianity to those without religious background. In the present volume, James' theological reflection creates a thoughtful reading center for the study of Romans, demonstrating how the former world can impact the latter.

# Foreword
Paul Scott Wilson

The problem with much preaching on Paul is that he is made to seem boring, turgid, AND abstract, like a talking head. His words in some hands seem to connect more easily with systems of abstract Christian thought than with the concrete lives and needs of ordinary people gathered to hear God's word. The problem is acute with Romans, for in this letter are many rich themes including sin, election and call, the faithfulness of God, justification by faith, the new creation, the eschaton, the law, and ethical outworking of the gospel. Preachers in the midst of their harried weeks and desperate for a sermon on Sunday can turn to Paul and find pithy verses that seem to speak immediate theological truths today. Moreover, they appear to break down easily into point form to facilitate a didactic form of sermon construction. Paul's vocabulary invites the mining of key doctrines in theology textbooks. The sermon too easily becomes an essay, and bewildered congregations who are ready to feed on the word of God find themselves suddenly instead in the midst of a seminary course, with the conversation going over their heads. Preachers, hoping to rekindle faith, find instead in drooping eyelids the seeming death sentence on their sermonic efforts.

That Paul comes to this in many pulpits is a lamentable irony, since Paul's ministry from beginning to end is pastoral in focus; Romans is a pastoral letter written to address real-life problems in specific churches. At the turn of the previous century in London, England, Alfred E. Garvie was offering lectures to groups of lay leaders on the subject of lay preaching. Though speaking about preaching in general, he defines with beauty and elegance one of the key challenges in preaching from Romans: "In the structure of the sermon, we must not only seek to assist the memory, but we must try also to stimulate the imagination. In order to do this we must ourselves not only conceive the truth as thought, but perceive it as life....the preacher should not conceive his message as doctrine, but perceive it as experience."[1]

This current volume contributes to preaching Romans as *experience*. In the year 49 AD, Emperor Claudius had exiled Jewish Christians. Now that Claudius is dead, the exiles have returned home after six years to their old house churches, and then, as now, old and new members may bicker. Everything Paul preaches stands for the unity of the body of Christ. James Walters shows that Jewish-Gentile tensions inform all of Romans; Paul's response as a pastoral theologian is to insist on the power of God for salvation for everyone who has faith, the Jews foremost. Seen from this perspective, chapters 5-8 offer a cosmic emphasis on salvation: a new age has been ushered into the old, and Christians are to "become what God is continuing to make [them]." For James W. Thompson, the older homiletic traditions tried to explain the text, its words and propositions, and the challenge today is both to read Romans as narratives about Paul, his congregation, and salvation, and to bring these narratives into conversation with our own stories. Stephen Farris takes on the tough problem of finding helpful analogies between Romans and today; he devises a series of

---

[1] Alfred E. Garvie, *A Guide to Preachers* (London: Hodder & Stoughton, 1906), pp. 239, 242.

questions to help preachers strengthen their own
sermonic analogies. Dave Bland offers Paul as a model for
the preacher as moral theologian. In Paul, community
formation takes precedence over the individual, and
moral vision for the church as a community in the image
of God takes precedence over preaching on specific
ethical issues that focus on cases rather than on building
character. Mark Love suggests that preachers learn from
*how* Paul uses Scripture: he does not preach *texts*, he
preaches the *gospel*. He uses theological imagination—
not a hermeneutical "bridge"—to read Scripture in
relationship to the cross. Following Paul's example,
preachers' imaginations will bring into play echoes and
allusions from Scripture, contemporary situations, and
implications of the cross and resurrection of Jesus Christ.

One's sermons from Romans will be better if one has
a vital sense that the ancient people are real people like
you and I. Gathered for worship, many await Paul's
words eagerly, prayerfully, expecting their communal and
individual lives to be changed, conformed to God's will.
Someone takes Paul's letter and reads a portion of it
aloud, perhaps chapter 8. A cool afternoon sea breeze
blows through the open door of the house, perhaps the
same breeze carrying Paul's ship at that moment to
Jerusalem. Hearing Paul's words read in their midst is like
hearing Paul himself speak to them, for these are his
thoughts phrased his way, addressed specifically to their
troubles. He says, Your groans in present suffering are
proof that you have received the first fruits of the Spirit.
When you are weak, and you do not know how to pray,
"the Holy Spirit intercedes with groans too deep for
words." All creation groans as it moves towards God's
mighty purposes. Christ Jesus is in the midst of your pain
and your groans are his groans. God hasn't stopped
working: the unity for which you long *is* the unity God
longs for you to have.

We cannot know the joy that such words brought those Roman churches. Perhaps alienated friends were awakened to a spirit of forgiveness; divided families began to dream of reconciliation. Whatever took place, we know that Paul's words made a difference to people's lives, and God used his words to powerful effect. He spoke to their hearts, and not just to their heads; he addressed issues that mattered.

The sermon examples in this volume do just that. They suggest that when our preaching has something of Paul's vitality and relevance—for which, like us, he ultimately depends upon the Holy Spirit—we are likely to be preaching Romans faithfully. Paul's words then will sound pastoral, concrete, helpful, and loving, speaking directly to life, sounding like experience born of faith.

# *Introduction*

David Fleer

Dave Bland

On Saturday evenings across the country devotees turn to Public Radio to hear the latest report from Lake Wobegon, where the men are good-looking, the women are strong, and the children above average. Although cast as humorous monologue, many listen because they long to have dormant emotions and spirits brought back to life. Through Garrison Keillor's narratives of temptation, dashed hope, or suppressed dreams, persons hear wondrous details which coincide with moments from their own experiences. Keillor's Lake Wobegon, from his 1985 novel to the latest radio update from St. Paul, creates a passionate and emotive world.

Some are drawn to Lake Wobegon because its fictive creation often includes plots and characters that resemble their own religious experiences. Consider Keillor's historical sketch of his church, the Sanctified Brethren, who a century before had broken away from the Anglican Church over matters of doctrine and morality. Keillor describes his fellowship this way:

> Once free of the worldly Anglicans, these fire brands turned their guns on each other. Scholarly to the core and perfect literalists everyone, they set to arguing....Once having tasted the pleasure

of being Correct and defending True Doctrine, they kept right on and broke up at every opportunity, until, by the time I came along, there were dozens of tiny Brethren groups, none of which were speaking to any of the others.[1]

Despite these argumentative origins, the preaching heard in Lake Wobegon is worth consideration. For example, after hearing a homily on self-denial, Keillor's adolescent narrator responds, "Ha! Easy for nuns to talk about giving up things. That's what nuns do for a living. But, I'm twelve, things are just starting to go right for me!"[2] Troubling sermons, passionate lives, and familiar church origins: Lake Wobegon has all of the elements of an engaging life.

Keillor and his world have had their detractors, however. Even Keillor himself appears to limit his work to humor, claiming, "*Wobegon Boy* is a prose entertainment, conceived after I had gotten an honorary degree from a college and sat and heard myself described as a giant and a vast force for good in our time. I didn't want to be that good. I only wanted to write stuff that would make readers laugh out loud...."[3] This appears to be an invitation to dismiss Keillor's serious reflection on grounds of either effect or motive. However, Keillor's affective stories, from that of a middle aged man's bout with depression to a teenager's sexual appetite, function not as appeals to entertainment lusts but as close readings of the human character intending to seriously engage listeners. Preachers should not so quickly discharge

---

[1] Garrison Keillor, *Lake Wobegon Days*, (N.Y.: Penguin Books, 1986), 130-131.

[2] Keillor, *Lake Wobegon Days*, 281.

[3] Katie Bolick, "It's Just Work: Garrison Keillor on Radio, Writing, and His Perpetual Revolt Against Piety," *Atlantic Unbound*, Interview, October 8, 1997 (www.theatlantic.com/unbound/factfict/gkint.htm).

Keillor, as he teases us to do, but study him as a champion of those who pay close attention to the world.[4]

Our tendency as preachers has been to move in toward the human heart through use of the language and tools of psychology, sociology, or politics. Keillor may be a helpful corrective for us. His created fictional world of Lake Wobegon turns to experience with his world to express deep emotion and honest spirituality. We propose, not that we use his fictive creation, making Lake Wobegon, as some have with Mayberry RFD, the location for interactive Sunday School discussion. Rather, we suggest that preachers of the Word absorb the passionate and emotive *biblical* narratives and learn to tell them with Keillor like texture and fullness.

This move, of course, is fraught with peril. In the days following the September 11 tragedies in New York City and Washington, D.C., thousands of preachers were catapulted into Sunday's pulpit needing to say a word from God. Even before Sunday dawned, Jerry Falwell had, with the assurance of an Old Testament prophet, judged that American Humanism was responsible for the devastation and death. Others found resources in apocalyptic literature or the psalms of revenge, connecting Washington and New York to Jerusalem.

In the wake of the September 11 tragedy, some preachers turned to more appropriate narratives, like that found in Job, whose story comforts those who live in the ambiguity of suffering and frees the sufferer to cry in anger and pain to God. For the preacher versed in the

---

[4] In the same interview Keillor reveals more of his purpose: "[*Wobegon Boy*] is a revolt against piety, I hope—against the sort of thing that Kathleen Norris and these holy midwesterners write, the heavy-breathing school of writers who go for long walks and look at sparkling reflections in the water and think about continuity and change. This book is supposed to be fun to read. Anyway, it was fun to write." The truth, of course, is that Keillor has examined his world with all the intensity of the heavy-breathing writers, with whom he contrasts his work.

genres of Scripture and the congregation schooled in the language and imagery of these stories written to help us understand how we think and what we feel, for a moment the church was able to transcend the politically charged atmosphere.

Stephen Carter cautioned us, before September 11, that political preaching turns to the Bible to find support for what it already believes.[5] Carter's warning still is true after the day of infamy: we must not turn the Bible into a proof text for our own created ideals. If the Christian first makes up his or her mind about what political or moral position to take and next searches the biblical text to support the predetermined view, the idea of biblical faith as the source of moral guidance is belittled. Listen, instead, to hear beyond our incensed emotions, a word from the Lord.

This is not to take the advice attributed to Karl Barth, "aim above the hill of relevance," and avoid in Sunday's sermon news from the week. Just the opposite! We comprehend *this* world through the reality of the world pictured in Scripture. Our effectiveness as preachers thus relies on our living in and describing the narratives given to us.

The easy prescription to go "Back to the Bible" is not so easily enacted, however. Indeed, we share the religious heritage of one of Keillor's narrators, a literal reading and militaristic application resulting in generations of church splits and wounded hearts. We have extracted from the text precisely what we came expecting to find. Thus, our desire is not to resurrect the same disastrous enterprise, but to set out in this series of books a

---

[5] Stephen L. Carter, *The Culture of Disbelief*, (N.Y.: Anchor Books, 1993), 81. Elsewhere Carter clarifies, "Bear in mind what is occuring. The group does not consult Scripture to determine whether or not the cause is just. Rather, the quotes are selected to prove the justice of the cause." Carter, 74.

means of surveying the intimate terrain of the world that promises transcendent meaning. In short, we hope that this volume will provide an appropriate model for the hungry preacher and hopeful congregation who search for the passionate realities found within the worlds revealed in Scripture.

The conceptual center of the present volume is the thesis set forth in James Thompson's chapter. Thompson claims that Paul's epistles provide a window to the apostle's preaching by repeating and continuing Paul's prior conversations. Thus, when one considers that Paul often wrote of future interactions with the recipients of his correspondence, the epistle is the middle part of a larger and living narrative. Like a still photograph, an epistle implies a related and larger story. One reason recent preaching has avoided Paul, Thompson suggests, is that we have missed the narrative behind his letters.

Thompson has long advocated a close and intelligent reading of the text, one that emphasizes theological, historical, and rhetorical concerns. Acknowledging that folk today have little appetite for "reasoned discourse," Thompson believes that Paul's theology, interwoven with pastoral concerns, can lead the church to reflect on its own story. Thompson's clear warning is this: without critical theological reflection, the church will mistake gospel for popular cultural ideologies. Thompson has spent his career unpacking New Testament scholarship for use in the church. He continues that project with his article in this volume, arguing that the preacher need not choose between preaching epistle and preaching narrative because the salvation story of Christ pervades Paul's thought in Romans and is the foundational narrative for all Christians.

How then does the preacher negotiate a reconstructed world of Romans with our own lives? Stephen Farris claims that a sermon is biblical when it coheres in likeness and similarity with the biblical world. For Farris, the way to link the world of the Bible with our world is through analogy. Farris asks us to search for fundamental similarities between the two worlds to foster an encounter between text and listener.

Farris knows that preaching is more than a didactic task to uncover meaning, a job that can be accomplished without reference to God. Since preaching aims to encounter God, preaching cannot occur without God's presence and power. Farris' thoughtful and stimulating work continues in the fourth chapter of this volume where he guides the reader into a theological exercise in analogical thinking. He conducts the preacher through a series of questions in order to help identify similarities and differences between the text in Romans 5:1-11 and contemporary American culture. For this passage, which focuses on the atonement of Christ, Farris offers insightful suggestions for those struggling with how to tell the story of the death and resurrection of Christ to people who often do not appreciate God's gracious act. How can a message, so foreign to a self-help culture, be heard?

Mark Love interacts with Farris' thesis by exploring the way in which Paul uses Scripture in Romans. Love looks to Paul as a model for preaching from Scripture. Focusing on Paul's use of texts, Love critiques the imbalanced emphasis on discovering the right method to bring the text into the contemporary world. Neither salvation nor effective preaching can be found in a proven scheme. Paul does not replicate a particular technique, Love claims, but a theological stance. Since the preacher is not a scientist but a practical theologian who uses Scripture to address congregational issues, Love argues that Scripture funds the imagination of the sermon.

Dave Bland pushes the theoretical discussion of the first half of the book toward praxis as he probes how

Paul's letter to the Romans informs the role of the preacher as moral theologian. Bland critiques the contemporary therapeutic culture and popular moral education movements in public education in light of Paul's theology. Paul speaks of the development of character in the context of a faith community and in the presence of a goal that is greater than any one individual. In the midst of a therapeutic culture, Paul calls Christians to an alternative faith community. Ultimately, preaching reminds the church that the task of moral development is not about our success or well-being. The task of moral development is focused on God's kingdom entering into a sinful and self-centered world.

With Thompson's chapter functioning as the conceptual center of this volume, James Walters provides the theological foundation. The distinguishing feature of Walters' construct is that justification by faith is not the primary issue in Romans. Rather, Walters argues that the central concern in Romans is the issue between Jew and Gentile. While justification by faith clarifies this relationship and sheds light on Paul's thought in Romans, the most essential concern is how Gentile Christians should treat the Jewish Christians returning to Rome after their expulsion by Claudius. Those welcoming the exiles are asked to understand the continuity of the law with the gospel and recall that God's covenant began with the Jews. Such a perspective should have a profound influence on the way in which one reads and preaches from Romans.

This volume concludes with a series of sermons by two preachers who have learned the narrative of Romans and tell it with textured fullness. Mike Cope and Ken Durham each write six sermons that are not just literary pieces but were first preached to their respective congregations in Abilene, Texas and Malibu, California. These sermons show the practical development of the theoretical suggestions of the volume's first half. They were born not only from the preachers'dialogue with the contributors to this volume, but with the book of Romans, the people in their congregations, and God. Cope and Durham demonstrate the practical results of reading closely the narrative world of Romans while paying rapt attention to the realities of the lives that surround them. To facilitate the interactive dialogue between Paul and his audience, Durham's sermons creatively employ two characters who "extend the conversation" beyond Paul's extant epistle. Cope uses more conventional forms to retain the epistle's narrative context.

The worlds of the Bible are the places where we are understood for our true selves, where we can discern our meaning and are encouraged to live above the mundane and self-absorbed. May this volume help transport the listener into a realm where he or she may be fashioned by the God who promises to recreate us all.

# I

Part 1:
*Texts, Themes,
and Issues in
Preaching Romans*

# 1

# Ethnic Issues, Eschatology, and Moral Reasoning in Paul's Letter to the Romans

James Walters

Paul's letter to the Romans is no doubt one of the most influential documents ever written. Arguably, no other single writing in the biblical canon has affected the history of Christian thought as dramatically. Reading Romans prompted major turning points in Christian history—Augustine, Luther, and Barth come quickly to mind—which profoundly influenced both western Christianity and western civilizations.

This essay is concerned with the theology of Romans in light of recent scholarship. No attempt is made to treat the theology of Romans in a complete, balanced, or systematic manner. Rather, the essay focuses on major issues or themes that have the potential to whisk those wishing to proclaim the message of Romans to the heart of the letter.

## Ethnic Issues and the Occasion and Purpose of Romans

Since Martin Luther and the Protestant Reformation, it has been routine to label "justification by faith" as the central theme of Romans with 1:16-17 viewed as thematic verses. Justification by faith is without question central to the development of Romans. However, making it the letter's chief concern is problematic. Although this theme figures prominently in the argument of chapters 1-8, it does *not* in chapters 9-16. Moreover, when justification by faith is made the central theme, chapters 9-11 are typically relegated to a secondary position—labeled a digression by some—even though the position of these chapters in the argument and their emotional appeal make them appear much more central to the letter's purpose.[1]

Although Romans 1:16-17 continue to be viewed by most scholars as thematic verses, there has been a decided shift in how these verses are read. Instead of interpreting justification by faith as Paul's chief concern (with Jew/Gentile issues appearing for illustrative purposes), Jew/Gentile issues are increasingly seen as the letter's central focus. The reason justification by faith is so important in the letter is because Paul believes it especially clarifies this relationship—as 1:16, 17 themselves suggest:

> For I am not ashamed of the gospel; it is the power of God for salvation to *everyone* who has

---

[1] A growing number of scholars consider chapters 9-11 to be the climax of the letter. See for example, J. Christiaan Beker, *Paul the Apostle* (Philadelphia: Fortress, 1980), 87.

faith, *to the Jew first and also to the Greek.* For in
it the righteousness of God is revealed through
faith for faith; as it is written, "The one who is
righteous will live by faith" (1:16-17, emphasis
added).

A clear indication that this emphasis on Jew/Gentile
issues is correct appears when one asks the following
question: In which of Paul's letters does justification by
faith play a prominent role? Romans and Galatians are the
only ones; and these are the very letters in which the
relation between Jews and Gentiles is the central issue
under consideration. It should be apparent then that
justification by faith is a key theme for Paul precisely when
he is discussing Jew/Gentile issues.[2]

Although justification by faith is prominent in both
Galatians and Romans, it is extremely important to
distinguish the context and argument of Romans from
that of Galatians with regard to Jew/Gentile issues.
In Galatians, the weight of Paul's argument rests on
Jewish Christians who were exercising power over
Gentile Christians. These Jewish Christians stressed the
continuity of the gospel with Judaism, finding in
Abraham a pattern for Gentiles within Judaism. J. Louis
Martyn imagines—based on the text of Galatians as well
as contemporary Jewish traditions regarding Abraham—
that the Jewish Christian opponents of Paul may have
spoken to the Galatian churches regarding Abraham in
the following manner:

What is the meaning of this blessing which God
gave to Abraham? Pay attention to these things:

---

[2] Arland Hultgren, *Paul's Gospel and Mission* (Philadelphia: Fortress Press,
1985), 93.

Abraham was the first proselyte. As we have said, he discerned the one true God and turned to him. God's blessing took the form, therefore, of an unshakable covenant with Abraham, and God defined the covenant as the commandment of circumcision. He also revealed to Abraham the heavenly calendar, so that in his own lifetime our father was obedient to the law, not only keeping the commandment of circumcision but also observing the holy feasts on the correct days. Later, when God handed down the law on tablets of stone at Sinai, he spoke once again by the mouths of his glorious angels, for they passed the law through the hand of the mediator Moses (Gal 3:19). And now the Messiah has come, confirming for eternity God's blessed law, revealed to Abraham and spoken through Moses.[3]

Martyn's reconstruction of the opponents' message reveals a line of continuity between Abraham, circumcision, the law, and the Messiah that Beker calls the "chain" argument of the Judaizers. It is an argument with a compelling conclusion: "Abraham's circumcision defines the domain of the messianic blessing in Christ and marks the proper line of salvation-history."[4] Consequently, Paul's discussion in Galatians 3 was designed to drive a wedge between Abraham and the law. By emphasizing the differences between the promise to Abraham and the law, Paul is able to show that God's

---

[3] J. Louis Martyn, *Galatians*, The Anchor Bible (New York: Doubleday, 1997), 303.

[4] Beker, *Paul the Apostle*, 52.

purposes do not flow in a continuous way from the law to Christ. This argument would clearly reduce the power Judaizers were able to wield over the Gentile Christians in Galatia by pointing out that what God was doing with the gospel was different from what God did with the law.

In Romans, on the other hand, the stress is on the continuity of the gospel with Israel and Israel's Scriptures—not discontinuity as in Galatians—and the weight of the argument rests primarily on Gentile Christians, not Jewish Christians. Paul's stress on the Jewishness of the gospel, or its continuity with Israel, is clear from the very beginning of Romans. Only in the salutation of the letter to the Romans does Paul describe the gospel in such starkly Jewish terms (1:1-7): not only was the gospel promised beforehand in the Jewish Scriptures, it is itself the story of a Jew (God's son "who was descended from David according to the flesh"). In 1:16 Paul describes the gospel as the power of God for salvation for everyone who has faith, *to the Jew first* and also to the Greek (see also 2:9-10). When Paul asks the rhetorical question, "Then what advantage has the Jew? Or what is the value of circumcision?" He answers, "Much in every way" (3:1-2). It has long been recognized that the law is described in much more positive terms in Romans than in Galatians. In Romans, Paul calls the law "holy and just and good" and "spiritual" (7:12, 14). Moreover, Christians who walk by the spirit "fulfill the just requirements of the law" (8:4).

The clearest evidence that Paul in Romans is determined to demonstrate the continuity of the gospel with Judaism is found in Romans 9-11, especially chapter 11. Paul denies that God has rejected Israel, starkly identifying himself as "an Israelite, a descendant of Abraham, a member of the tribe of Benjamin" (11:1). In direct address to Gentile Christians, he chastises them for their arrogance against Jews by pointing out that they had been grafted as "wild olive shoots" into an olive tree that is indisputably Jewish (11:11-24). And then, in a striking exclamation, Paul writes,

> So that you may not claim to be wiser than you are, brothers and sisters, I want you to understand this mystery: a hardening has come upon part of Israel, until the full number of the Gentiles has come in. And so all Israel will be saved... (11:25-26).

Some have denied that Paul's use of the term "Israel" carries any ethnic connotations here. However, his explanation for God's continuing commitment to "Israel" is based on the promises God made to the patriarchs: "...the gifts and the call of God are irrevocable" (11:29). In Romans 14:1-15:13, the well-known passage about the "weak" and the "strong," Paul places primary responsibility upon the strong who were mostly Gentile Christians. Although the weak are exhorted not to judge the strong, it is the strong who are directed to alter their behavior so that the weak—those who refrain from meat or who keep special days—will be able to live on the basis of their own faith (14:20-23).[5] When referring to the collection he was gathering from Gentile churches for poor saints in Jerusalem, Paul claims that the collection is appropriate because Gentiles owe a debt to the Jews: "if the Gentiles have come to share in their (the Jews') spiritual blessings, they (the Gentiles) ought also to be of service to them in material things"

---

[5] On the identity of the "weak" and "strong" in this text and the focus of Paul's argument, see James C. Walters, *Ethnic Issues in Paul's Letter to the Romans* (Valley Forge, Pa.: Trinity Press International, 1993), 84-92.

(15:27). In the letter's personal greetings, Paul describes two Jewish Christians, Prisca and Aquila, as persons for whom not only he but also "all the churches of the Gentiles" give thanks (16:3-4). Moreover, Paul goes out of his way to point out the Jewish identity of a missionary couple whom he says were Christians even before he was (16:7).[6]

Paul's desire to stress the gospel's continuity with Israel can also be seen in the way arguments are based in Romans: whereas arguments in Galatians are built primarily on the basis of claims regarding Christ (christological arguments), arguments in Romans are more often based on claims regarding God (theological arguments). Sampley has pointed out that in Romans Paul speaks of

> God's righteousness (1:17), God's wrath (1:18), God's judgment (2:2), God's kindness (2:4; 11:21), God's love (8:39), God's severity (11:21), God's gifts and call (11:29).... In the same way, the questions that focus Paul's reflection are questions that center upon God: "is God unjust to inflict wrath on us?" (3:5); "Has the word of God failed?" (9:6); "Is there injustice on God's part?" (9:19); "Has the potter no right over the clay?" (9:21); and "Has God rejected Israel?" (11:1). By contrast to all these questions concerning God and God's purposes, there is only one question about Christ in all of Romans (8:34).[7]

---

[6] On this couple, see James Walters, "Phoebe and Junia(s)—Rom 16:1-2, 7," in *Essays on Women in Earliest Christianity*, ed. Carroll Osburn (Joplin, Mo.: College Press, 1993), 185-90.

[7] J. Paul Sampley, "Romans and Galatians: Comparison and Contrast," in *Understanding the Word*, essays in honor of Bernard Anderson, ed. J. Butler, E. Conrad, B. Ollenburger (Sheffield: JSOT, 1985), 322-23.

It should be apparent that the argument of Romans differs significantly from that of Galatians.[8] Although Jew/Gentile issues and justification by faith figure prominently in both Galatians and Romans, the differences between these two letters are striking and must be kept in mind by interpreters. Scholars in recent years have attempted to account for the Roman letter's emphasis on the Jewish character of the gospel by focusing on a convergence of two sets of issues: those relating to circumstances within the Roman Christian communities and those relating to Paul's own circumstances. This has increasingly led scholars to refer to "reasons" for Romans, rather than a single or dominant reason that accounts for the letter's content.[9]

I have argued elsewhere that Paul's decided emphasis on the Jewishness of the gospel in Romans is due in part to the development of Christianity in the capital from origins within the Jewish communities of Rome to house churches that were independent of Jewish synagogues.[10] This means that earliest Christianity in Rome would originally have been more Jewish in its socialization—Jewish dietary laws and Sabbath-keeping would have been the norm—than it was when Paul wrote Romans. It is also likely that the Claudian edict of 49 C.E. that evicted many Jews from Rome—including Christian Jews like Prisca and Aquila (Acts 18:2)— hastened this evolution of Christianity in Rome by reducing the numbers and influence of many of its Jewish members just prior to Paul's writing of Romans. When the evicted Jews returned to Rome after the death of the emperor Claudius—as Prisca and Aquila did

---

[8] For more on these differences, see Beker, *Paul the Apostle*, 94-108.

[9] Hence the book by A. J. M. Wedderburn, *The Reasons for Romans* (Edinburgh: T& T Clark, 1988).

[10] Walters, *Ethnic Issues in Paul's Letter to the Romans*.

(Rom 16:3-4)—they would have found house churches that were less Jewish in their socialization than before and less willing to make room for Jewish scruples.[11]

It is difficult to determine with certainty whether differences over dietary laws and observance of special days were responsible for some of the separate house-church groupings reflected in Romans 16. However, because of the tendency for such practices to serve as boundaries, it is likely that some house-churches in Rome were more law-observant than others, especially in the aftermath of the Claudian edict and the return of expelled law-observant Christians. If so, Romans 14:1-15:13 can be seen as the practical climax of the argument Paul made in Romans 9-11: Gentile Christians in Rome must not reject Jews; rather they must, by their behavior, make it possible for Jewish Christians to continue to be Jewish within their communities. It is Paul's prayer for the Christians in Rome that they discover such "harmony" among themselves that God may be praised with "one voice" (15:5-6)—not a Gentile voice and a Jewish voice. Although this "voice" must be unified, Paul makes it very clear that its unity must not be found at the expense of God's promises to Israel. Consequently, the burden is placed on the "strong" to make room for the "weak" (15:1). Thus Paul demonstrates in practical terms his commitment to protect the priority of the Jews against presumptuous Gentile Christians in Rome who seem to have forgotten that the olive tree is Jewish (11:17-24).

Paul's own context was similarly complex. He wrote Romans at a critical nexus in his missionary career. In the letter itself, the apostle informs his readers that his work

---

[11] Ibid., 59-62, 66.

in the East (from "Jerusalem to Illyricum," 15:19) is finished. His much-anticipated journey to Rome represents a new missionary horizon. However, Paul's trip to Rome—and his plan to proclaim the gospel in Spain—must wait for one final task in the East: he must return to Jerusalem because there is too much at stake in the delivery of the Jerusalem collection to entrust its success to others.[12] Because this relief project symbolizes Paul's commitment to one church of Jews and Gentiles (Rom 15:26-27), the Jerusalem church's acceptance or rejection of the Gentile Christian gift will be tantamount to a verdict on Paul's Gentile mission.[13] Paul was justified in his concern that the Gentile collection might be rejected by Jewish believers because many of them were convinced that his (law-free) gospel accomplished the inclusion of Gentiles at the expense of the identity of God's elect people.[14]

Over the past fifty years, the occasion and purpose of Romans has been the topic of considerable scholarly debate.[15] Space does not permit a detailed analysis of this question but some brief comments are in order. I am

---

[12] Paul no doubt viewed the delivery of the collection as his fulfillment of an agreement he had reached with leaders in Jerusalem regarding what would be required of Gentiles in Paul's missionary endeavors (see Gal 2:10).

[13] See James Dunn, *Romans*, Word Biblical Commentary (Dallas: Word, 1988), 879-80.

[14] Jacob Jervell argued that Romans should be viewed primarily as a rehearsal of how Paul would defend his gospel to Jewish opponents in Jerusalem when he delivered the collection (Jacob Jervell, "The Letter to Jerusalem," in *The Romans Debate: Revised and Expanded Edition*, ed. Karl P. Donfried (Peabody, MA: Hendrickson Publishers, (1991), 53-64.

[15] The variety of viewpoints is well represented in *The Romans Debate: Revised and Expanded Edition*. However, for the best introduction to a variety of contemporary interpretive issues in Romans, see *Pauline Theology*, vol. 3, ed. David M. Hay and E. Elizabeth Johnson (Minneapolis: Fortress, 1995).

convinced that Romans was occasioned by Paul's desire to press westward in his mission to the Gentiles with the support of the Roman congregations. Because of Paul's avowed commitment not to build on the foundations of others (Rom 15:20), it is unlikely that he would have written to the Roman Christians if they did not figure into his westward mission.[16]

This rather straightforward occasion gave rise to an elaborate document because Paul's circumstances and those of the Roman Christian communities were complicated. Romans 1:8-13 and 15:14-29 indicate that Paul hoped to secure Roman support for his mission to Spain. However, this would have required some degree of mutual agreement and understanding among the Roman Christians regarding Paul's mission and gospel. It is worth noting that Romans is addressed to "God's beloved in Rome," not to the "church" in Rome as is more typical for Paul's salutations. Moreover, analyses of Romans 16 suggest that there were five to eight different house churches in Rome that likely differed in ethnic makeup and perspective.[17] Analysis of the letter suggests that Christianity in Rome was not unified and that the issue dividing believers was the very one that had made Paul's mission controversial among Jews from Jerusalem to Rome; namely, that Paul's gospel reflected insufficient regard for Jewish practice and identity. Hence, in Romans Paul must expound the righteousness of God in such a manner that both the universality of the gospel—it is the power of God for salvation for *everyone* who has faith—

---

[16] Leander Keck, "What Makes Romans Tick," in *Pauline Theology*, Vol. 3, 22.

[17] Peter Lampe, "The Roman Christians of Romans 16," in *The Romans Debate: Revised and Expanded Edition*, 216-230.

and the priority of Israel—it is for the Jew *first*—are protected. If successful, his argument would quiet Jewish Christian concerns regarding his gospel and deflate Gentile Christian boasting, without compromising the universality of the gospel. Success in this task would result in a more unified and sympathetic base of support for Paul's westward mission and Christian communities in Rome that reflected the unity among Jews and Gentiles that God sought (Rom 15:7-13).

Therefore, when one looks east to Jerusalem, west to Rome, and farther west to Spain, it is apparent that the ethnic issues Paul faced at this juncture in his ministry do in fact converge. In order for Paul's ministry to be acceptable in Jerusalem, common criticisms of his gospel must be apologetically engaged and the continuity of his gospel with God's purposes for Israel must be demonstrated. In Rome the same are required if common ground is to be established between Jewish and Gentile Christians because a Gentile majority assumed— or acted as if—God had elected Gentiles to take Israel's place. Furthermore, a successful mission to Spain demands that Paul present the Roman Christians with a clearer picture of his gospel and missionary enterprise; otherwise, he risks another mission plagued by the same uncertainty he now faces in Jerusalem. The document that resulted from these overlapping concerns is perhaps best described as a defense of God's covenant faithfulness to Jews and to Gentiles in the gospel.[18] The goal of this

---

[18] "Covenant faithfulness," as the central meaning of the "righteousness of God" in Romans, first advanced by Käsemann, has now been widely accepted (Ernst Käsemann, "'The Righteousness of God' in Paul," in *New Testament Questions of Today* (London: SCM, 1969), 168-82). "Covenant faithfulness" has become the connecting thread for N. T. Wright's interpretation of Paul. For a concise introduction to Wright's view, see "Romans and the Theology of Paul" in *Pauline Theology*, 30-67 along with Hays' critique of Wright (and Keck) in the same volume, 68-86.

defense is clearly stated by Paul in the conclusion of the body of the letter:

> Welcome one another, therefore, just as Christ has welcomed you, for the glory of God. For I tell you that Christ has become a servant of the circumcised on behalf of the truth of God in order that he might confirm the promises given to the patriarchs, and in order that the Gentiles might glorify God for his mercy (Rom 15:7-9).[19]

## Romans 5-8 and the Role of Eschatology in Romans

Once readers recognize just how pervasive Jew/Gentile issues are in Romans, a fresh reading of the letter is apt to generate new questions about chapters 5-8 and particularly the role of these chapters in the argument of Romans. Whereas Romans 1-4 and 9-11 are peppered with ethnic terms (Jew, Israel, Gentile) and 53 quotations from Israel's Scriptures, in Romans 5-8 Paul does not use the terms Jew, Israel, or Gentile even once and quotes Scripture only twice.[20] How does one account for this dramatic difference?[21]

---

[19] See Donaldson's argument that 15:7-13 is the concluding summary of the body of the letter (*Paul and the Gentiles*), 95-100.

[20] Frank Thielman states this difference clearly, but attempts to play it down, in an essay entitled "The Story of Israel and the Theology of Romans 5-8," in *Pauline Theology*, Vol. 3, ed. David M. Hay and E. Elizabeth Johnson (Minneapolis: Fortress Press, 1995), 169.

[21] How one accounts for the differences between Rom 1-4 and 5-8 often indicates whether one takes a "salvation history" approach to the interpretation of Paul or one that emphasizes the revelation of the gospel as an apocalyptic event that represents the "newness" or "unexpectedness" of God's saving act in Christ. The former approach places greater emphasis on the

The common explanation for this shift since the Reformation has been to suggest that two different theological themes account for the differences. Whereas chapters 1-4 focus on justification, chapters 5-8 are concerned with sanctification. In other words, the difference is one of subject matter.

However, Ernst Käsemann's insight that the "righteousness of God" in Romans is Paul's way of expressing the notion of God's "covenant faithfulness" has resulted in scholars increasingly seeing both Romans 1-4 and 5-8 as expositions of God's righteousness.[22] According to this reading of the letter, it is not the subject matter that changes, but rather the perspective.[23]

The topics Paul treats in both sections are the universal character of sin, the role of the law, and the effects of the death of Christ. The topics even appear in basically the same order of progression in the two

---

*continuity* of the gospel with Israel's history while the latter approach stresses *discontinuity*. Charles Cousar describes the difference well when he writes:

> The issue is not whether Paul draws on the language and texts of the Old Testament (that is a given) but whether there is a discernible line of continuity between Israel's story in the past and the death and resurrection of Christ or whether the apocalyptic character of God's disclosure in Christ precipitates an irreparable rupture in the story that makes any smooth notion of continuity difficult to discern. In the latter case, the inbreaking new age is seen as a radical alternative to the old, rather than its sequel ("Continuity and Discontinuity: Reflections on Romans 5-8," *Pauline Theology*, vol. 3, 196).

On these contrasting approaches, compare the essays by Thielman and Cousar in *Pauline Theology*, vol. 3, 169-195 and 196-210, respectively (and the bibliography cited there).

[22] The well-known article where Käsemann advanced this view is "'The Righteousness of God' in Paul," in *New Testament Questions of Today*, 168-82.

[23] E. P. Sanders, *Paul and Palestinian Judaism* (Philadelphia: Fortress, 1977), 502-504.

sections. Therefore, it is reasonable to conclude that Paul covers roughly the same ground, but from a different perspective. In chapters 1-4 the perspective is forensic or juridical, while in chapters 5-8 the perspective is experiential and participatory. The difference of perspective between the two sections with regard to the topics they treat is instructive. As Donaldson has noted, whereas the universal character of sin is directed toward human culpability—"all have sinned"—in chapters 1-4, in chapters 5-8, sin is a universal power enslaving *all* human beings. Whereas the law is a means of establishing human guilt in chapters 1-4, it dramatizes the power of sin to enslave in chapters 5-8. Whereas the death of Christ is the means by which God justifies the ungodly in chapters 1-4, it is something in which believers participate in chapters 5-8, thereby freeing them from the dominion of Adam.[24]

Although traditionally Paul's understanding of salvation (his soteriology) has been explained especially in light of the forensic perspective of Romans 1-4, a shift is clearly underway in contemporary scholarship.[25] Donaldson's comment certainly reflects the trend in Pauline studies: "I take chaps. 5-8 to lie closer to the heart of Paul's soteriology than 1-4, his starting point in the earlier chapters being determined by rhetorical factors

---

[24] Donaldson, *Paul and the Gentiles*, 133. Wright attempts to minimize the distinction between 1-4 and 5-8 by arguing that justification in Paul—including Romans 1-4—is not about "how people enter the covenant," but a "declaration that certain people are already within the covenant" (Wright, "Romans and the Theology of Paul," in *Pauline Theology*, vol. 3, 66).

[25] This is one aspect of a larger shift in Pauline studies typically referred to as the "New Perspective" on Paul, prompted in large measure by Sanders' book, *Paul and Palestinian Judaism*. For a concise—and helpful—introduction to the "New Perspective," see Terrence Donaldson, *Paul and the Gentiles: Remapping the Apostles' Convictional World* (Minneapolis: Fortress Press, 1997), 3-27.

rather than the structure of his developed understanding of the gospel."[26]

When Romans 5-8 is given this kind of emphasis, the apocalyptic character of Paul's gospel comes to the forefront, and the view of salvation that results is less oriented toward the individual and more oriented toward creation. Although referring to a different Pauline text, Richard Hays' comments regarding the translation of 2 Corinthians 5:17 provide a helpful commentary on the implications of this shift for interpretation:

> The apocalyptic scope of 2 Corinthians 5 was obscured by older translations that rendered the crucial phrase in verse 17 as "*he is* a new creation" (RSV) or—worse yet—"*he is* a new *creature*" (KJV). Such translations seriously distort Paul's meaning by making it appear that he is describing only the personal transformation of the individual through conversion experience. The sentence in Greek, however, lacks both subject and verb; a very literal translation might treat the words "new creation" as an exclamatory interjection: "If anyone is in Christ—new creation!" Paul is not merely talking about an individual's subjective experience of renewal through conversion; rather, for Paul *ktisis* ("creation") refers to the whole created order (see Rom 8:18-25). He is proclaiming the apocalyptic message that through the cross God has nullified the *kosmos* of sin and death and brought a new *kosmos* into being.[27]

---

[26] Donaldson, *Paul and the Gentiles*, 337, n. 98.

[27] Richard Hays, *The Moral Vision of the New Testament* (San Francisco: Harper Collins, 1996), 20.

A brief analysis of the progression of the argument
of chapters 5-8 and the role of this section in the larger
argument of Romans will highlight the unique character
of these important chapters. As noted earlier, ethnic terms
(Jew, Israel, Gentile) disappear from view in this portion
of Romans. Paul's shift to a more cosmic perspective in
Romans 5-8 causes ethnic terminology to recede from
view. Because Paul is determined in this section to group
all human beings—whether Jew or Gentile—in Adam or
in Christ, the question of where one stands in relation
to the law of Moses or Israel is transcended by a larger
question, the question of God's redemption of the
creation. This larger question allows Paul to present the
cosmic scope of God's work of justifying the ungodly.[28]
This perspective provides Paul with a framework that is
more conducive to addressing the present and future of
salvation (what God is doing and will do) as well as
answering questions relating to the situation of believers
vis-à-vis sin and the law.

Romans 5:1-11 serves as a transition between the
two perspectives of chapters 1-4 and 5-8 with strong
connections to both what precedes and what follows.[29]
Paul makes it clear in 5:1-11 that because of Christ's
redemptive work believers have peace with God and
every reason to be hopeful about the future—in spite of
present sufferings. Because God is no longer an enemy,

---

[28] On this point, see especially Ernst Käsemann, *Commentary on Romans*,
translated by Geoffrey Bromiley (Grand Rapids: Eerdmans, 1980), 131-57.

[29] For connections to ch. 1-4, see C. E. B. Cranfield, *Romans*,
International Critical Commentary (Edinburgh: T & T Clark, 1975), 1:253.
That 5:1-11 actually belong to the material that follows was shown by Nils
Dahl who emphasized the connections between 5:1-11 and chapter 8 in
*Studies in Paul* (Minneapolis: Augsburg, 1977), 81-90.

believers can confidently depend on God as an ally in their present and future struggles toward final salvation. Although Paul can assure believers that their conflict with God has ended, his reference to "our sufferings" in 5:3 indicates that another source of conflict still exists. Explaining the cosmic dimensions of this continuing conflict in the context of God's redemptive work is his next order of business.

Paul clarifies the nature of the struggle Christians face in 5:12-21 by introducing two rival solidarities or dominions: Adam and Christ.[30] Sin reigns over all human beings because Adam's trespass was a cosmic disaster that unleashed sin in the world with the result that it spread to all human beings—because they all sinned (5:12). Notice how Paul speaks here of "sin" as a power that reigns, rather than "sins" as individual misdeeds.[31] Sin reigned even before Moses gave the law. When the law arrived on the scene, it exposed the dominion of sin by making it possible to quantify transgressions (5:12-14)—with the ironic result that it actually served to *multiply* them (5:20). Against this dominion of death, typified by Adam, Paul juxtaposes the (even more potent) dominion of life, typified by Christ. Associated with Adam are sin, death, trespass, condemnation, and disobedience while their opposites—grace, life, righteousness, justification, and obedience—are associated with Christ. The resurrection of Christ makes it clear to Paul that the dominion of life is more powerful than the dominion of death. Therefore,

---

[30] Although Adam does not explicitly enter the discussion until 5:12-21, his presence is increasingly seen as implicit already in 1:18-3:20 (Richard Hays, "Adam, Israel, Christ," in *Pauline Theology*, vol. 3, 74).

[31] As Dave Bland points out in his chapter, a therapeutic culture emphasizes individualism. In this mindset, the origin of "sin" is within each individual who must excise it through therapeutic resources. This stands in stark contrast to Paul's thought.

Paul is confident that increases in sin will be met by even greater increases of grace (5:20).

This last claim raises an objection to Paul's gospel noted already in 3:8, but not faced squarely until now: "Should we continue in sin in order that grace may abound?" Or to put it another way, does Christ's victory over sin and death render human obedience irrelevant? Paul answers, "By no means!" The gist of Paul's argument in chapter 6 is that since Christians are no longer "in Adam" but are "in Christ," their new identities must be reflected in their lives. Since Christians have shared in Christ's death by their baptism and have been raised to walk in "newness of life"—while awaiting their own "resurrection like his"—any continuation of a life dominated by Adam is unthinkable. Christians no longer live "in Adam," under the dominion or reign of sin, and must not therefore permit sin to regain a foothold in their lives.

Although this language is familiar to many Christians, the eschatological assumptions that stand behind it are not as familiar. Paul's contrast between these two rival dominions, his description of their character, and the way he portrays God as destroying the old age and establishing a new age shares much with Jewish apocalyptic eschatology. In fact, Beker claims that the "apocalyptic world view is the fundamental carrier of Paul's thought."[32] Although Paul wrote no apocalypse—the Revelation of John is the only apocalypse in the NT—comparisons with other apocalyptically-oriented materials help to clarify the unique character of Paul's outlook. Jewish apocalyptic scenarios typically depicted two successive ages: an evil

---

[32] Beker, *Paul the Apostle*, 181. For Beker's larger discussion of Paul's apocalyptic eschatology, see *Paul the Apostle*, 135-181.

age in which the righteous inhabit a corrupted earth and suffer great hardship, followed by a new age in which God reigns over a new heaven and a new earth. The transition between these two ages awaits God's dramatic action—what the book of Revelation describes and for which the community responsible for the Dead Sea Scrolls was waiting in the Judean desert.[33]

Paul's eschatological outlook differs significantly, however, from other apocalyptic schemes. Unlike the Dead Sea community, Paul was not waiting for God's dramatic action; he believed it had already occurred in the death and resurrection of Jesus. Nonetheless, he also believed that God's redemptive work was not yet fully complete because the old age (Adam) had not met its end (see 1 Cor 15:20-28).[34] Paul makes it clear that the reign of Adam/sin predated the reign of Christ/grace, but now describes them as concurrent dominions. It is in fact their overlapping status that explains the ambiguity believers experience in the present—joy and suffering, freedom from sin and assault by sin—an ambiguity reflected in the warnings and admonitions of Romans 6. Although those who have been baptized are *already* "in Christ," sin continues to look for an opportunity to reestablish Adam's dominion in their lives, indicating that they are *not yet* out of Adam's reach. The experience of believers confirms that sin continues to be a potent force in the world. The remainder of the argument in chapter

---

[33] On Jewish apocalyptic outlooks, see esp. John J. Collins, *The Apocalyptic Imagination* (New York: Crossroad, 1987).

[34] World War II analogies are sometimes used to distinguish what the death and resurrection accomplished from the conflict that continues until the second coming of Christ: The death/resurrection of Christ is D-Day while the second coming is V-Day (Beker, *Paul the Apostle*, 159-60).

6 drives home Paul's point that those in Christ cannot/must not permit sin to reign in their bodies.

Romans 7 dramatizes the enslaving power of sin as Donaldson has pointed out:

> Chapter 7 as a whole picks up and amplifies the description of the Adam solidarity introduced in 5:12-21. Consequently it covers the same ground as 1:18-3:20, but from the perspective of the actual subjective experience of human existence under sin and law, not the perspective of the objective status of sinful humanity before God.[35]

One way Paul dramatizes the enslaving power of sin in chapter 7 is by using the first person singular ("I" instead of "we," "you," or "they") to communicate the bondage of life in Adam and the law's impotence in the face of the dominion of sin.[36] Although Paul is clear that the law is "holy," "just," "good," and "spiritual" (see 7:12, 14), he is just as clear that the law is powerless before sin, unable even to prevent its own exploitation by sin (see 7:8, 11). Believers are not bound to the law (7:1-6); however, their hope does not rest in their freedom *from* the law, but in the *dominion of Christ*. Why or why not? Because the fundamental issue is not the law, but sin.[37]

The limits of the concurrent dominions (Adam/Christ) are finally clarified in chapter 8 as Paul explains how the Holy Spirit assists believers in their struggle with sin. Those who are in Christ have their

---

[35] Donaldson, *Paul and the Gentiles*, 135.

[36] See especially James Dunn, *Romans*, 1:381-83.

[37] This is why Anders Nygren's characterization of the theme of Romans 7 as "Freedom from the law" is misleading (*Commentary on Romans* [Philadelphia: Fortress, 1949], 265-303).

minds set on the Spirit and walk according to the Spirit. Consequently, they fulfill the "just requirement of the law" (vv. 1-8). The Spirit dwelling in Christians bears witness that they belong to God even while they await their final resurrection that will be accomplished through the Spirit of "him who raised Jesus from the dead" (vv. 9-11). In the meantime, those who have been adopted by God reject the power of the flesh, putting "to death the deeds of the body" by the power of the Spirit (vv. 12-17)—the same Spirit that also attests to their identity as children of God.

Romans 8:18-25 are the most critical verses in the entire letter for unpacking the eschatological drama that informs Paul's discussion. This paragraph describes Christians—even the whole creation—living in hope of final redemption. The sufferings of the "present time" are contrasted with the "glory about to be revealed to us." The creation was "subjected to futility" and since that time has been in "bondage to decay"—a clear reference to the cursing of the ground in the Genesis story of Adam's fall. Those in Christ, who have the "first-fruits of the Spirit," as well as the creation itself, groan like a woman in childbirth as they await final redemption.[38] Although not stated explicitly in this text, both the liberation from bondage anticipated by the creation and the "redemption of our bodies" (8:21b, 23b) will take place at the Second Coming of Christ (see 1 Cor 15:23).

---

[38] The pains of childbirth provide an excellent analogy for an apocalyptic outlook. Unlike other types of pain, labor pains are good news and indicate that the sufferer is getting ever closer to joy and freedom. The patient must understand clearly what is going on—a point not lost on either natural birth instructors or apocalyptic authors—because otherwise the patient would assume she was getting closer and closer to death instead of life. The sufferings of believers, therefore, do not indicate that God's efforts for a new creation have failed. On the contrary, because these pains are birth pains, they offer assurance that the new creation is already underway and proceeding right on course.

This is when Adam's influence finally ends. Human beings, no longer possessing bodies like Adam, are no longer under the threat of sin exploiting them through their bodies—Adam will no longer have any opportunity because God will be "all in all" (1 Cor 15:28).[39]

For Paul, God's future reign has *already* broken into the present with the death and resurrection of Christ. Those who are in Christ *already* participate in that reign even while still having bodies like Adam. Consequently, even though they are no longer under the dominion of sin, they are *not yet* outside of sin's reach. Those who are "in Christ" were *formerly* slaves of sin but are *now* slaves of righteousness. Although they have *not yet* experienced the redemption of their bodies, they have *already* received the Spirit that attests their divine adoption and enables them to put to death the deeds of the body. Hays captures well the eschatological tension: "To live faithfully in the time between the times is to walk a tightrope of moral discernment, claiming neither too much nor too little for God's transforming power within the community of faith."[40] Consequently, Paul attempts to teach his converts the art of "walking between the times."[41]

## *Eschatology and Ethics*

Since Bultmann's classic essay, "The Problem of Ethics in Paul," the rubric of the "indicative and

---

[39] It is important to remember that redemption for Paul does not equal an escape from the body, but rather a redemption of the body itself. Paul does not have as low a view of the body as some have maintained. See Dunn, *The Theology of Paul the Apostle*, 55-72.

[40] Hays, *The Moral Vision of the New Testament*, 27.

[41] The carefully chosen title of Paul Sampley's book on the apostle's moral reasoning (*Walking Between the Times: Paul's Moral Reasoning* [Minneapolis: Fortress, 1991]).

imperative" has been recognized as basic to interpreting Pauline ethics.[42] Because the relationship between the indicative and imperative in Paul's moral exhortation is closely related to the apostle's eschatological outlook described above, we are in a good position to explore this aspect of Pauline ethics.

The "indicative" refers to Paul's declarative statements regarding God's redemptive work in Christ, including not only the salvific event of the cross/ resurrection, but also God's initiation of the "new creation" by means of that event. The "imperative" describes the responsibility of human beings to reflect in their own lives—and in the life of the community—the in-breaking of God's new creation.

Once this structure is recognized, it becomes clear that the relationship between the indicative and imperative is not a haphazard one in Paul. For Paul, the indicative always precedes the imperative; they are not reversed. This pattern is reflected in the common "therefore" constructions in Paul: God has done "X"; therefore, believers must do "Y." The relationship between the indicative and imperative is evident when one compares Rom 6:1-4 and 6:5-14. The progression between the two paragraphs is essentially "you have died with Christ" (vv. 1-4, the indicative); "therefore, consider yourself dead" (vv. 5-14, the imperative). It is apparent that what God has done through Christ is the necessary precondition for what those "in Christ" are able to do.[43]

The importance of this structure and its nuances can be illustrated by comparing texts from other Pauline

---

[42] Victor Furnish, *Theology and Ethics in Paul* (Nashville: Abingdon, 1968), 9.

letters. Paul accuses the Galatians of confusing the relation between the indicative and the imperative by asking them, "Are you so foolish? Having started with the Spirit, are you now ending with the flesh" (Gal 3:3)? By requiring Gentile Christians to be circumcised and keep the law, Paul is convinced that his opponents have placed the imperative ahead of the indicative. Reversing the order of the indicative and imperative results in grounding salvation in human effort, effectively nullifying the grace of God (Gal 2:19-21).

It is also reflected in Colossians 3:1: "Since you have been raised with Christ (indicative), seek the things that are above" (imperative). This passage is a direct response to opponents whom Paul accuses of attempting to establish the indicative by promoting imperatives like "Do not handle, do not taste, do not touch" (2:21). Paul wonders why the Colossian believers, who have already died with Christ (indicative, 2:20), would resort to behavioral imperatives to establish what had already been accomplished for them by God's redemptive act in Christ.

The importance of maintaining the proper relationship between the indicative and the imperative is dramatically illustrated in 1 Corinthians 5:6-8. In a text where Paul is pressing the Corinthians to expel a man who is living with his father's wife, he reverses the order of the indicative and imperative. He tells them to "Clean out the old yeast (imperative) so that you [the Corinthians] can be a new batch" (indicative). However, he immediately follows the exhortation with an important corrective: "as you really are [already] unleavened. For our paschal lamb, Christ, has been sacrificed" (1 Cor

---

[43] Dunn, *The Theology of Paul the Apostle*, 629.

5:7). Paul quickly clarifies that the Corinthians do not in fact have the capacity to establish an "unleavened" status before God by removing the immoral man from their midst. They can only reflect the "unleavened" status God has given them through Christ's sacrifice.

The imperative has sometimes been called the human response to the indicative. Although this protects the proper order, it still fails to communicate the integral relationship that exists between the indicative and the imperative in Paul. If separated, the imperative becomes merely the means by which one "actualizes" what God only made a "possibility" through the indicative.[44] The phrase "become what you are" has been suggested as a kind of shorthand for the Pauline imperative that protects the integral connection between the two.[45] Dunn is correct that "become what you are becoming" may better reflect the eschatological tension in Paul.[46] However, "become what God is continuing to make you"—though not as catchy—better represents both the eschatological tension that characterizes the believer's experience in Christ and also the continuing dependency of the believer on redemptive power.

Two texts in the letter to the Philippians illustrate the importance of these nuances for Paul. In Philippians 1:6, Paul makes it clear that God has not turned over full responsibility for the imperative to those who have been justified. He assures the Philippians that "[God] who began a good work in you will bring it to completion at the day of Jesus Christ." The integral relation between the indicative and imperative—the initial and continuing

---

[44] Furnish, *Theology and Ethics in Paul*, 225.

[45] Though Furnish has questioned whether it in fact does so (Ibid.).

[46] Dunn, *The Theology of Paul the Apostle*, 631.

dependency of the believer on redemptive power—is probably best reflected in Phil 2:12b-13: "Work out your salvation with fear and trembling; for God is at work in you, both to will and to work for his good pleasure."

That Paul's moral reasoning assumes the structure of the indicative and imperative—with its connection to eschatology—can be seen in other texts in Romans. A noteworthy example involves Paul's comments about the renewal of the mind in Rom 12:2. When Paul exhorts the Roman Christians not to be conformed to "this world/age" but to be "transformed by the renewing of your minds," his eschatological assumptions are evident. Conformity to "this world/age" would be submitting to the dominion of Adam, while the "renewing of the minds" reflects the "new creation" that has broken into the present by virtue of Christ's death and resurrection. For Paul, those who have rejected the knowledge of God have minds that are "darkened" or "base" (Rom 1:21, 28).[47] Those who are "in Christ" are in the process of having their minds renewed so that they are becoming increasingly able to figure out or discern the will of God (Rom 12:2b).[48] Therefore, those who are "in Christ" continue to experience God's creative power by which they are losing their conformity to "this world/age," even while still living in it. However, because Christians live in the interval between the death/resurrection of Christ and the *parousia*, all human action is predictably flawed to some degree. The *not yet* affects and conditions human ethical possibilities in the *now*. Therefore,

---

[47] See 2 Cor 3:14, 15 where Paul contrasts those who have minds that are hardened or veiled with those who are "being transformed into the same image from one degree of glory to another."

[48] Sampley, *Walking Between the Times*, 55.

what can be expected of individuals and institutions—including churches—must be adjusted accordingly.[49]

---

[49] Dunn, 629-30.

# 2 | Narrative Preaching from Romans
### James Thompson

The preacher's task, according to good homiletic theory, is to communicate the ancient text to the contemporary audience. Like many other ideals, this one is not always easy to put into practice. Some passages—especially the weighty texts in the epistles—present us with such a daunting prospect that we scarcely imagine bridging the gulf between the text and our listeners.

I learned long ago that my listeners connected more easily with narratives than with the epistles. Narratives sustain interest, provide anticipation, and allow listeners to identify their personal stories with those of the participants in the biblical narratives. Even old and familiar stories maintain their power to engage the interest of the congregation. When I attempted to preach epistles, on the other hand, I struggled to elicit the same level of rapport with the congregation that I had found with stories. The epistles seemed to me to be abstract, intellectual, and lacking the narrative dimension that the listeners appreciated. Thus my experience confirmed what narrative theologians have insisted: that we learn the truth of our own existence through the medium of story.[1] Like many other preachers, I discovered that the preaching of epistles presents a special challenge for one who recognizes the vital importance of narrative. This problem becomes especially acute when we recognize that twenty-two of the twenty-seven books of the New Testament are epistles, for it raises the question of the extent of our preaching canon.[2]

My experience was typical of a generation of preachers. With the rise of the "new homiletic" in the 1970s, the focus on narrative inevitably relegated the epistles to the periphery of the preaching canon. Whereas the older homiletic tradition, with its focus on "getting an idea across," was comfortable with the theological content of the epistles, advocates of the new homiletic focused on narrative. The dense theological arguments of the epistles did not appear to fit our fascination with story. We assumed that the listeners could more readily connect with the healing of blind Bartimaeus, for instance, than with Paul's arguments about justification by faith, sanctification, or the destiny of Israel (Rom 9-11).[3] Consequently, the canon confronted the preacher with this dilemma: to

---

[1] On the significance of narrative in answering our basic worldview and moral questions, see J. Richard Middleton and Brian J. Walsh, *Truth is Stranger Than It Used to Be* (Downers Grove, Ill: Intervarsity, 1995), 63-66.

[2] For the purposes of this article, I include Revelation and Hebrews. Revelation, with its introductory letter to seven churches, has an epistolary component. Although Hebrews may best be described as a homily, it has an epistolary ending.

[3] See James W. Thompson, *Preaching Like Paul* (Louisville: Wesminster John Knox, 2000), 15.

preach narrative and maintain listener interest or not to preach narrative and lose the audience.

This dilemma is especially crucial when we consider the possibilities of preaching Romans. All of the epistles present a challenge, but Romans is a special challenge. We are likely to be incredulous of Karl Barth's claim that Romans is an open letter to the twentieth century, for we find its style and its ideas difficult for the contemporary audience. We have been influenced by the traditional Protestant reading of Romans, according to which the epistle is "the compendium of Paul's theology," and we read it to discover propositional statements. We associate Romans with the profound doctrinal statements that have influenced Protestant theology for centuries. One can imagine, for example, preaching on Romans 3:21-26, a passage filled with dense theological argumentation.

> But now, apart from law, the righteousness of God has been disclosed, and is attested by the law and the prophets, the righteousness of God through faith in Jesus Christ for all who believe. For there is no distinction, since all have sinned and fall short of the glory of God; they are now justified by his grace as a gift, through the redemption that is in Christ Jesus, whom God put forward as a sacrifice of atonement by his blood, effective through faith. He did this to show his righteousness, because in his divine forbearance he passed over the sins previously committed; it was to prove at the present time that he himself is righteous and that he justifies the one who has faith in Jesus.

This passage, a restatement and elaboration of the thesis of the book (1:16-17), is the ultimate challenge for the preacher. No passage in the New Testament is so dense with theological statements. It is especially daunting to anyone who has actually worked through Romans in a graduate course, for exegetical work makes one aware that every phrase in Romans 3:21-26 is not only profound, but also disputed territory. The discussion in the graduate seminars has taught us how complex are the ideas that Paul treats in Romans. Consequently, in preaching this passage in Romans, we recall the academic debates over each phrase. The "righteousness of God"—is it a subjective or objective genitive? Is Paul describing *righteousness* as an attribute of God or as a gift that God imputes to humankind? We also recall that, whereas most translations render *pistis christou* as "faith in Christ" the phrase is actually, "faith (or faithfulness) of Christ" (3:22), and that exegetes continue to debate the translation. Whereas the NRSV renders *hilasterion* (3:25) as "sacrifice of atonement," older translations render the word either as "propitiation" or "expiation."

In the older homiletic tradition, the task of the preacher was to explain the text. The preacher would explain the difficult words of the text in the course of a sermon on the atonement and then apply the message to the audience. One does not preach long, however, before recognizing that one's listeners are not sitting on the edge of their seats expecting to hear an explanation of *dikaiosyne tou theou, pistis christou* or *hilasterion*! We may begin the task of preparation by picturing the faces of the listeners. The teenagers sit on the second row. On a good day, we involve them in the sermon, but on other days their minds are elsewhere. Further back are the parents who are distraught over their inability to communicate with their grown children and barely able to concentrate on the service. A widow has returned to church for the first time after losing her husband of forty-five years. Then there are the numerous people in the congregation who almost did not come. In addition to the individual stories that we recall in our own communities of faith, we think also of our specific congregational story. We face the tensions between young families, who want us to focus our ministries on their children and those who want us to focus on the elderly. Our congregation has an uneasy peace over the style of the worship service. The assembled congregation, therefore, comes in expectation, not of an academic discourse on Pauline theology, but of a word that helps make sense of their own lives. The preaching of Romans becomes a special challenge.

If we think of the preaching task as one of explaining propositional statements to an audience that is attentive primarily to stories, we have an impossible role. However, I suggest that *this is not our task*. We do not choose *between* preaching epistles and preaching narrative, for the epistles themselves participate in a larger narrative involving the convergence of stories. We find in the text the *convergence* of Paul's story, the story of the listeners that lies behind the text, and the story that brought the church into existence. The preacher engages the text by bringing the story of the congregation into dialogue with the narrative of the text.

Preachers educated in historical criticism have learned that letters participate in a narrative, recognizing the importance of placing every statement within the epistles within a historical context, which is the story behind the letter. More recently, scholars have pointed beyond the historical narrative behind the text to the "narrative world" that is implied within the text.[4] Every letter has the essential elements of a story—point of view, plot, and closure.[5] Paul is the narrator who supplies the point of view, the plot, and the anticipated ending of the story. Although we do not know if the anticipated closure occurred as Paul planned (his anticipated visit or reunion with his churches), the epistles project an end to the story. The epistles are a portion of an ongoing conversation between Paul and his listeners, and the interpreter's task is to interpret the plot that the letter reveals. Paul's dense theological arguments are actually woven within a story and come to life only when we acknowledge the surrounding story. Like a still photo, the epistles freeze one moment in time within a larger story in which Paul addresses an ancient congregation. As with every still photo, multiple stories lie behind the photo, and multiple stories lie in front of it. In the epistles we recognize Paul's story and the story of his listeners. To preach is to bring our own story into conversation with these texts.[6]

---

[4] See Norman R. Petersen, *Rediscovering Paul: Philemon and the Sociology of Paul's Narrative World* (Philadelphia: Fortress, 1985), 14.

[5] Ibid., 14-15.

[6] Thompson, *Preaching Like Paul*, 40.

## *Paul's Story in Romans*

Paul does not write the epistle as an exercise in academic theology, but as a response to a crisis, both in his own life and in his churches. In Romans, for example, we can discover the narrative world within the epistle. As Paul writes, he has reached the turning point in his tumultuous ministry. Since his call to apostleship, he has preached the gospel throughout the eastern Mediterranean basin in a circle "from Jerusalem to Illyricum" (15:19). With this reference to the geographical expanse that he has covered in his ministry, he has summarized a story of many years' duration. His statement that he has wanted for a long time to visit the Romans (1:13; 15:22) also suggests a narrative of Paul's lengthy ministry and his relationship with the listeners. His story is not over, however. Having often wanted to come to Rome (1:13; 15:22), he now plans to make that long-awaited journey, and then to complete the circle of his missionary journeys by going on to Spain (15:24). He now faces a major crisis as he completes his plans. Having gathered a collection for the saints of Jerusalem from his Gentile congregations, he now hopes to deliver the collection that will communicate the unity of the Jewish and Gentile churches (15:25-27). As he writes Romans, he is uncertain of his reception in Jerusalem. He asks the Roman church to pray that he may be delivered from the unbelievers of Judea and received favorably by the believers of this region (15:30-32). The reception of this gift will signify the fulfillment of his mission as an apostle. If Paul's plans go well, he may then proceed to Rome, followed by a trip to Spain with the help of the

Roman church. Behind the epistle to the Romans, therefore, one discovers a story. In fact, as Paul dictates Romans to his amanuensis (16:22), he is in the middle of a story that awaits completion, a story that he projects into the future. We do not know the full outcome of the story that Paul anticipates. Although we know from Acts that the unbelievers in Jerusalem did not receive him, we do not know if the believers accepted the contribution. We are left with the story that Paul envisions for the future. This letter, like other Pauline letters, cannot be separated from the story that lies behind and in front of it. Behind every statement in Romans is the story of Paul's missionary labors.

Although Romans lacks the elements of Paul's personal story that one finds in Philippians or 2 Corinthians, Paul alludes to the story of his life and destiny at numerous points. When he indicates that he is "called an apostle" and "set apart for the gospel of God" (Rom 1:1), he alludes to the event that transformed his life and determined his destiny.[7] In 9:1-5, he compares himself to Moses as he describes his personal anguish over the condition of Israel and his willingness to be cursed for the sake of his own people. When he states clearly near the end of the letter that he has written "because of the grace given me by God to be a minister of the Gentiles, so that the offering of the Gentiles may be acceptable, sanctified in the Holy Spirit" (15:15-16), he suggests that his personal

---

[7] Although many interpreters have understood 7:7-25 as an autobiographical reflection, the "I" is best understood as a literary convention describing the human condition apart from the power of the new age. For the literary convention, see Stanley Stowers, *A Rereading of Romans* (New Haven: Yale University Press, 1994), 258-59.

narrative is one part of a larger story of God's mission to the world, and that he is God's instrument for this purpose. The purpose of Romans, at least in part, is to explain Paul's personal story, including his missionary labors.

## The Story of the Listeners

Paul's story intersects with the narratives of his listeners. As Romans 16 indicates, Paul's listeners come to the community with many stories. One may assume that they, like Aquila and Priscilla, have brought their own personal narratives to Rome from other communities throughout the Roman Empire (see 16:2-3). The list of names in Romans 16 suggests the variety of individuals and groups within the Roman church, all of whom have brought their personal and national stories. Some of the listeners are Jews and others are Gentiles. Some are slaves or freedmen. The fact that the listeners assemble in different house churches in Rome probably suggests that they come from different socio-economic groups.[8] The house churches include men, women, and presumably children.

Because all of the ethnic groups found their way to Rome, the city and the church represent a great challenge. Although Paul refers only obliquely to the

---

[8] On the house churches of Romans, one may note the reference to the church in the house of Aquila and Priscilla (Rom. 16:5). For further information on the house churches of Rome, see Francis Watson, "The Two Roman Congregations: Romans 14:1-15:13," and Peter Lampe, "The Roman Christians of Romans 16," in Karl Donfried, ed., *The Romans Debate* (Peabody, Mass.: Hendrickson, rev. ed. 1991. See also James Walters, *Ethnic Issues in Paul's Letter to the Romans* (Valley Forge: Trinity, 1993).

situation of the Roman church at the time of this writing, we can ascertain considerable information about this church. The description of the strong and the weak in Romans 14:1-15:13 may suggest that Paul is responding to recent events in the Roman church. The fact that Paul moves from "strong" and "weak" (14:1; 15:1) to "Jews and Gentiles" (15:7-8) suggests that the underlying problem of Romans is an ethnic dispute in which different house churches were not welcoming each other into their respective communities. Paul's references to the problems of boasting, arrogance, and a judgmental attitude (cf. 2:1; 3:27-4:2; 11: 16-25; 14:1-5) indicate that arrogance was undermining the harmony between the ethnic groups within the church.[9]

Claudius' expulsion of the Jews from Rome in AD 49 (cf. Acts 18:1-2) may provide the background of this tension. Jewish Christians left Rome, and probably returned to Rome only after the death of Claudius (AD 54).[10] The returning Jewish Christians would have discovered a church that had changed in their absence. This new situation probably created a conflict between a Gentile church with its own distinctive character and set of memories and the returning Jewish Christians, who brought their own memories. Therefore, in addition to the individual stories represented in the Roman church, the rival groups probably had their own competing versions of the Christian story and practices. If Romans is a response to a difficult

---

[9] For the occasion of Romans, see Karl P. Donfried, "False Presuppositions in the Study of Romans," in Karl P. Donfried, ed., *The Romans Debate*, 102-24.

[10] See W. Wiefel, "The Jewish Community in Ancient Rome and the Origins of Roman Christianity," in *The Romans Debate*, 85-101.

situation, it is not the "compendium of Paul's theology," but a sermon addressed to Christians who were a part of a continuing drama.

The purpose of Romans is to effect change in the Roman church and to ensure that the house churches do not remain in separate enclaves, but that they welcome one another as Christ has welcomed them. In 15:5, Paul concludes his argument with the prayer that the Christians "be of one mind." In 15:7, he indicates that the conclusion of his argument will bring the two groups to "glorify God with one voice." Thus the entire argument about justification by faith is a challenge to the Roman church to lay aside the arrogance that destroys community.

Recent scholarship recognizes the vital importance of the relationship between the narrative framework of Romans (1:1-17; 15:14-16:16) and the dense theological argument in the body of the letter. This theological section is actually an answer to the questions facing Paul and the Roman church. The theological section, as Paul indicates in Romans 15:15, is intended to justify Paul's ministry. Through the medium of theological discourse, Paul declares that "all have sinned" and that God saves "all"—both Gentiles and Jews—through his righteousness; that is, the theology shapes the outcome of the story of the Roman church. Despite the different stories that are represented in the Roman church, "all" share the story of creation and fall. If we recognize that each pericope in Romans is a response to a critical issue in the life of the church and a statement intended to affect the conclusion of the church's story, we will no longer regard the statements as abstractions far removed from our listeners.

## *Paul and the Story of Salvation*

If Paul's task is to bring the rival communities to "glorify God with one voice" (15:6), Romans is the still photograph in this continuing drama. As Paul indicates in Romans 15:15-16, Israel's story provides the framework for his own personal narrative. His statement that he is the "minister of God to the Gentiles" presupposes a narrative that culminates in Israel's mission to the Gentiles. The story began, as Paul indicates, with the creation of the world, the disobedience of the first man (Rom 1:20; 5:1-12; 7:7-25), and the spread of sin to all humanity (1:18-3:20; 5:12-21), leaving both Jews and Gentiles without a reason to claim superiority. The narrative continued in the call of Abraham, who would become the father of a new humanity composed of Jews and Gentiles (4:3-22), and through his immediate descendants, Isaac and Jacob, whom God elected to serve his purposes (9:6-13). It included Moses (9:14-18), the exodus,[11] the giving of the law (5:13-14), Israel's rebellion and exile. Paul shares Israel's hope for God to demonstrate his righteousness and to complete the restoration of the people from exile and the fulfillment of the promises which God made to Abraham.[12] With Israel, he looks forward to the restoration of the primordial situation before the fall (Rom. 8:18-29) and

---

[11] See N. T. Wright, "New Exodus, New Inheritance," in *Romans and the People of God*, ed. Sven K. Soderlund and N. T. Wright (Grand Rapids: Eerdmans, 1999), 28-31. Wright argues that the reference to baptism in Rom. 6:4 is a reminder of the crossing of the Red Sea and that the references to "redemption" (3:24), slavery, and freedom (6:12-19) reflect Paul's Christian reinterpretation of the exodus story.

[12] See Frank Thielman, "The Story of Israel and the Theology of Romans 5-8," in *Pauline Theology III: Romans* (Minneapolis: Fortress, 1995), 182-83.

the future occasion when "all Israel will be saved" (11:26).

Although Jewish listeners would have claimed the biblical narrative as their own, Paul insists that it belongs to both Jews and Greeks. Gentile Christians can look to their pre-Christian condition as the result of the sin of the one man, and they may look to Abraham, Isaac, and Jacob as their ancestors (9:6-13). Similarly, the story of Christ is the shared narrative of both Jews and Gentiles. Thus, because of the profound events that have shaped his life, Paul both assumes and subverts Israel's story, recalling the narrative through the lenses of the Christ event. As N. T. Wright says, "We can see how Paul's brief, often clipped, references to Jesus function within the letters as mini-stories, small indices of the rudder by which the great Jewish narrative world had been turned in a new direction."[13] Consequently, Romans, like other epistles of Paul, is filled with mini-stories about Jesus, the culminating figure of Israel's story. Although Paul does not write gospels, he tells the story of Jesus, which becomes the point of orientation for all of his theology.

> "…who was handed over to death for our trespasses and was raised for our justification." (4:25)
> "For while we were still weak, at the right time Christ died for the ungodly. Indeed, rarely will anyone die for a righteous person—though perhaps for a good person someone might actually dare to die. But God proves his love for

---

[13] N. T. Wright, *The New Testament and the People of God* (Minneapolis: Fortress, 1992), 407.

us in that while we still were sinners Christ died for us." (5:6-8)

"The death he died, he died to sin, once for all; but the life he lives he lives to God." (6:10)

"For God has done what the law, weakened by the flesh, could not do; by sending his own Son in the likeness of sinful flesh, and to deal with sin, he condemned sin in the flesh." (8:3)

"For to this end Christ died, and rose again, so that he might be the Lord of both the dead and the living." (14:9)

"For Christ did not please himself...." (15:3)

"For I tell you that Christ has become a servant of the circumcised on behalf of the truth of God in order that he might confirm the promises given to the patriarchs...." (15:8)

Romans, like all of Paul's epistles, assumes the story that the people already know. The story of Jesus Christ is both the culmination of Israel's story and the defining story for the new Gentile converts. In Christ, the sin of Adam is undone and the covenant with Abraham reaches its goal.[14] In Christ, God's righteousness extends not only to Israel, but to the Gentile converts as well. Just as "all" are under God's wrath because of the pervasiveness of sin, God's righteousness is also "for all who believe." Thus the death of Christ, the foundational story for the two rival groups in Rome,

---

[14] N. T. Wright, "Romans and the Theology of Paul," in David M. Hay and Elizabeth Johnson, *Pauline Theology III: Romans* (Minneapolis: Fortress, 1995), 46.

has undermined the arrogance of both groups and placed them together in a covenant relationship with God. Both groups are the recipients of the long-awaited "redemption" (3:25), and Christ is, again for both groups, the "expiation" for their sins (3:24). We may note in Romans 15:1-9 that Paul draws explicitly on what was known of the ministry of Jesus as the basis for the appeal he is making,

> which in fact plays a larger role within the purpose of Romans than is usually recognized: the different backgrounds of the various Christians in Rome should not prevent them from uniting in common worship. 15.3 and 15.7-9 speak of the ministry which the true Messiah undertook, recognizing his proclamation to Jews as a distinct stage in the outworking of God's universal purposes.[15]

The coming of Jesus is the turn of the ages, the climax of God's story that now awaits completion. Paul claims that Jesus Christ has brought about the peace and restoration envisioned by the prophets. Within the community of faith, he sees the fulfillment of Jeremiah's promise of a new covenant in which the people of God would fulfill the demands of the law (Rom 8:4). Among those who believe, the promise of Jeremiah is now fulfilled (see Jer 31:31-34).

Although the new has come, Paul recognizes that both the church and the creation itself still await the end of the story (8:18-39). In fact, whereas the first four chapters of Romans describe the past events that have shaped the Christian community, chapters 5-11

---

[15] Wright, *The New Testament and the People of God*, 408.

indicate that the community shares a corporate story that is not yet finished. This story then becomes the community's story as they share the foundational story. Paul says,

> Do you not know that all of us who have been baptized into Christ Jesus were baptized into his death? Therefore we have been buried with him by baptism into death, so that, just as Christ was raised from the dead by the glory of the Father, so we too might walk in newness of life. For if we have been united with him in a death like his, he will certainly be united with him in a resurrection like his. (Rom 6:3-5)

At the present, they live with unfulfilled hopes. Paul awaits the conclusion of the story when the mission to Jews *and* Gentiles will be complete, and Jews and Gentiles will praise God *together*.

All of the Christians in Rome have been united with Christ in baptism, and together they have received the story of the cross as their own story. Insofar as they have been "united with him in the likeness of his death," they have united with each other in "newness of life" to live together in a shared ethical response to the righteousness of God.

The story of the Roman community is not over. As Paul demonstrates in 5:1-10 and 8:18-39, they share with the whole creation the expectation of the final consummation of God's purposes. In the meantime, they live between the "now," in which there is "no condemnation" (8:1), and the "not yet" of the final triumph of God. They have experienced the power of the new covenant announced by Jeremiah, according to which they will fulfill the demands of the law through the Holy Spirit who has equipped them to live before the end.

As Paul indicates in 15:15-16, he has a significant place in God's plan, for Paul has received a special grace to be the apostle to the Gentiles. He recalls especially the language of the exilic prophets (Isa 49:1-6), according to whom Israel's story will reach also to the Gentiles. In the collection of funds for the poor saints in Jerusalem, Paul hopes to demonstrate the coming of the treasures of distant lands into Zion.

Because Jews and Gentiles stand together as recipients of God's righteousness, neither group has the basis for arrogance or boasting. Neither do the Gentile Christians have a basis for arrogance, for God will ultimately redeem the Jews also. At the end of the story, God will reclaim his entire creation, and "all Israel will be saved" (11:26).

## *Romans and the Story of our Churches*

To preach Romans is not only to bring together the stories of Paul, the Roman church, the Old Testament, and the earliest Christians, but also to bring our own stories into dialogue with the ancient story. The power of epistles once written to specific situations is that they continue to address communities that share the problems faced by the ancient churches. Just as the story behind Romans illuminates the tension between different cultures that had difficulty glorifying God with one voice, we continue to face similar problems. Like the Roman church, we discover that a church composed of others who are different from ourselves creates problems. The presence of others, who come with different memories, stories, and traditions, is sure to create tensions. Consequently, as the sociologists point out, the homogeneous church offers the opportunity for security, stability, and outreach. In the homogeneous church, we are likely to share the same tastes and expectations. Because people are uncomfortable crossing the boundaries of class and color, the Sunday assembly may be the one hour of the week when we are most isolated from those who are different from us. Thus our situation intersects that of Paul's listeners.

We see the challenge of bringing together different groups to "glorify God with one voice" in the tensions that are present within congregations. We face barriers, not only between ethnic and socio-economic groups, but among a variety of subcultures as well. In some instances, the conflict emerges when suburban sprawl results in the encounter between rural churches and the new members who have come from the suburbs. In other instances, church leaders agonize over how they can satisfy the competing demands of "boomers," "busters," and the older members of the church. The battle over worship styles is but one example of the barriers between rival groups within the church.

Churches commonly face these tensions by creating zones of homogeneity, wherein each group ensures the maintenance of its own comfort level and maintains its distance from others. Just as the Roman church was composed of separate house churches in which the natural response of the Christians was to remain within the separate house churches and maintain separation from others, we often respond to diversity within the church by discovering ways to maintain the separation between the cultures through enclaves of like-minded people. Although the churches of significant size will find a need for encouraging the development of smaller groups in order to minister effectively, these small groups often interact little with the corporate community. Worship services and other activities that are designed to meet separate tastes contribute to our natural desire to live within our own comfort zone, but *they do not demonstrate the power of the gospel to unite us in fellowship with those whom we did not choose.*

## To Glorify God with One Voice

The preacher's task is not to celebrate our homogeneous churches, but to bring different groups together so that they can overcome the natural human tendency to remain within their own subculture. We bring them together by demonstrating that we share a common story of the one who "did not please himself." As we declare that the "righteousness of God [is] through faith in Jesus Christ for all who believe" (Rom 3:22), we recognize that our own group does not have a monopoly on God, but that God's righteousness extends to those whom we did not choose. Paul's language about the righteousness of God challenges our own security and self-assurance and challenges us to see that these great doctrinal statements have a cutting edge that has not grown dull, even in our own time. The fact that "*all* have sinned" and that salvation is "for *all* who believe" is our permanent reminder that Christ's love builds a new kind of community.

The reading of Romans has been the source of theological revolutions throughout the history of the church. The letter, with its call for rival groups to come together as a new kind of community, is a summons to the church of all ages to demonstrate the power of the gospel to change lives and to recognize that God created a community composed of those whom we did not choose. Romans continues to challenge us to recall that "the righteousness of God is for all"—even those whom we did not choose.

I wish to reclaim Romans for the pulpit, where it belongs. It was meant to be *read in church*, not to be dissected in the graduate seminar. Our task of reclamation begins with the fact that we do not choose between preaching epistles and preaching stories, for the epistles are still photos of an action that awaits completion. Like the listeners of past ages, we come to Romans looking for the answer that will reshape us into a new kind of community where people of diverse backgrounds can "glorify God with one voice" (15:6).

# 3

# *Paul's Ethics in the Letter to the Romans:*

## Preaching that Forms a Moral Community
### Dave Bland

The church often remains oblivious to cultural forces that influence its thoughts and actions. Today, a therapeutic mindset emphasizing individual needs over community values drives much of our culture. The success and self-fulfillment of the individual become the focal point. Appearance and personality, for example, frequently override character and integrity.[1] A therapeutic culture believes that individuals possess within themselves all the resources necessary to heal their psychological and emotional infirmities. One needs little assistance from outside sources, let alone God. Individuals devote their energy to finding the available means within to gain relief from tension, emotional discomfort, and frustration. Little interest or energy remains for obligations to others.

The major problem is the church's response. Rather than setting out to offer an alternative community, the

---

[1] For further development of this cultural shift, see David Wells, *Losing Our Virtue: Why the Church Must Recover Its Moral Vision* (Grand Rapids: Eerdmans, 1998).

church frequently succumbs to reflecting the therapeutic mindset. Robert Wuthnow observes that spirituality now primarily concerns itself with providing therapy.[2] No longer do people look to the church, Scripture, or God to tell them what choices to make, but to tell them that the choices they have *already made* are okay.

In the past few years in this country, public education has initiated a renewed interest in moral instruction.[3] Does the renewed effort, however, offer viable hope to a society immobilized by terror, riddled with immorality, and driven by the therapeutic? Or does it simply reflect another dimension of the therapeutic mindset? In such a climate, the church looks to the preacher to assess the surrounding culture and proclaim a vision of God's community based on the gospel.

This chapter describes Paul's approach to moral instruction as he deals with the thorny relationship between Jews and Gentiles in his letter to the Romans. Using Paul's theological paradigm, I want to critique the philosophy and practice of the current character education movement that many schools, organizations, and churches incorporate into their curricula. I also want to reflect on how Paul's theology informs the role and responsibility of preaching ethics in the context of the contemporary church.

---

[2] Robert Wuthnow, *God and Mammon in America* (New York: Free Press, 1994), 5.

[3] See James Davison Hunter, *The Death of Character: Moral Education in an Age Without Good or Evil* (New York: Basic Books, 2000), 3-4, 107ff.

## Paul and the Letter to the Romans

James Thompson noted that one of the tasks of preaching is to bring a disparate group of individuals together to shape them into a community that reflects the image of God.[4] In reflecting his image, individuals become a community of high moral character. But how does preaching contribute to this process? In his letter to the Romans, Paul presents a paradigm for understanding the task of the preacher as moral theologian.

To be sure, Paul's letter is not a moral tract. Paul's primary concern is not a particular moral agenda. But embedded within the larger agenda of his letter are issues of proper moral conduct among believers. Preachers who earnestly desire to offer moral direction for their churches need to understand Paul's larger agenda in writing to the Romans before they can faithfully proclaim a Christian ethic.

In writing his letter, Paul encourages the homogeneous house churches that meet in Rome to accept one another as brothers and sisters in Christ in order to glorify God (Rom 15:5-6). The one community consisted of distinct house churches that existed throughout the city.[5] Each house church appears to maintain a distinct identity.[6] For example, Paul refers to the "churches of the Gentiles" in 16:4 without rebuking them for

---

[4]  See chapter two in this volume.

[5]  Five to eight house churches are mentioned in Romans 16, according to James Walters' count. See chapter one in this volume.

[6]  This is not unlike the phenomenon described in Acts 6 where synagogues with distinct identities seemed to exist. Luke refers to "the synagogue of the Freedmen" (possible reference may also be made to a synagogue of the Cyrenians and Alexandrians; Acts 6:9). Homogeneous churches and synagogues seemed to be accepted by the New Testament writers.

maintaining their cultural distinction. At this point, what Paul asks of these churches needs clarification. According to Richard Oster, Paul was not out to meld the house churches and different ethnic groups in Rome into one homogeneous whole; rather he wanted Jews and Gentiles to respect their differences and accept one another in Christ (15:7).[7]

Paul maintains that they must not unite on the grounds of ethnicity, but rather on the grounds of their relationship with Jesus Christ. Paul's task is to call two distinct cultures, Jew and Gentile, who had little respect for each other, to share together in a common faith.[8] Their oneness will then reflect a particular Christian lifestyle that manifests itself in the way they talk about each other, behave toward one another in the course of daily affairs, and share their financial resources with other saints (Rom 15:25-29). Thus, the moral character of individual Christians will be modeled after the larger faith community of which they are a part.

## *The Problem in Rome*

Paul is quite aware that the Christians in Rome are experiencing major difficulties. During the reign of

---

[7] See Richard Oster's article for a succinct argument on the diverse religious culture that existed in the churches in Rome. Oster, " 'Congregations of the Gentiles' (Rom 16:4): A Culture-Based Ecclesiology in the Letters of Paul," *Restoration Quarterly* 40, no. 1 (1998): 39-52.

[8] One needs to realize that Paul was not trying to blend two cultures together in worship and unity. The issue is not the integration of house churches. The issue is accepting one another in Christ, while respecting cultural diversity (Rom 14-15). While I deeply respect the insight and scholarship of James Thompson in the previous chapter, I disagree with his perspective that Paul was trying to break up the homogeneous house churches.

Claudius, the emperor had expelled the Jews from Rome around AD 49 (Acts 18:2; see earlier remarks by James Walters). But about six years later in AD 55, the year following Claudius' death, the Jews had been allowed to return.[9] The problem was that, during those six years, the Gentiles had become the dominant power in the church. With the Jews returning, the Gentiles had reservations about the place of the Jews in the church. There was tension between the two groups regarding their religious and cultural practices (Rom 14-15).

Paul writes the letter to address the problem and to bring about unity in the community. Paul believes that there is room for both groups; each can honor its own cultural heritage without jeopardizing oneness in Christ. Because they are united in Christ, they must express that unity in the way they conduct themselves. Certain behavior is expected from them, regardless of cultural differences. It is in this context that Paul engages in moral discourse. In overhearing this discourse, the preacher as moral theologian learns the role and function of ethical conduct in the Christian community.

## The Place of Moral Discourse in Romans

For Paul, the development of character takes place in the context of a faith community and in the presence of a goal that is greater than any one individual. Paul does not present a systematic treatment of Christian ethics anywhere in his writings. "Instead," according to Richard Hays, "he responds ad hoc to the contingent

---

[9] James Dunn, *Romans,* Word Biblical Commentary, vol. 1 (Dallas: Word Books, 1988), liii.

pastoral problems that arise in his churches."[10] The occasion generates particular moral demands; "specific pastoral problems in Paul's churches elicit his theological reflection."[11] Paul's *theology* drives his *ethics*. As Stephen Farris has affirmed in the next chapter of this book, Christian doctrine *creates* Christian identity. The two are interrelated.

Paul's moral theology flows out of the story of what God has done for his people. His theology uses an indicative/imperative paradigm. By indicative I mean that he tells the story of the redeeming actions of God in Christ manifested in the new life of believers. By imperative I mean that he describes the ongoing responsibility of believers to live out this new life in Christ. The relationship between the two establishes the framework for Paul's ethics.[12]

Romans 12-15 contain the heaviest concentration of moral imperatives in Romans. Perhaps because of this fact, the relationship of chapters 12-15 to the rest of the letter has been a matter of debate. According to Hays, "Martin Dibelius...proposed that the blocks of moral advice that occur at the end of Paul's letters should be understood as *parenesis*, general collections of maxims adopted from popular Hellenistic philosophy."[13] Dibelius suggests that Paul added the paraenetic section later, when Christ did not return immediately, in order to offer

---

[10] Richard Hays, *Moral Vision of the New Testament* (New York: HarperCollins, 1996), 17.

[11] Ibid., 18.

[12] See Michael Parsons, "Being Precedes Act: Indicative and Imperative in Paul's Writing," in *Understanding Paul's Ethics: Twentieth Century Approaches*, ed. Brian S. Rosner (Grand Rapids: Eerdmans, 1995), 217-47.

[13] Hays, 17.

guidance for a longer period of "exile" in this world. So the paraenesis in Romans 12-15 is not integral to Paul's gospel. Instead the chapters "recycle a general moral wisdom widely shared in Hellenistic culture."[14]

Contrary to Dibelius' view, however, no solid evidence exists to confirm that Paul tacked on chapters 12-15 as an afterthought. Rather than speculating about how Paul responded to the delay of the parousia, it is better to deal with the material as it stands and to understand the theological context of the paraenetic section in light of the whole letter. Paul inextricably weaves his exhortations into the Christian story. His moral imperatives flow out of the gospel he proclaims in the first eleven chapters.

With Paul, the reader witnesses a constant dialectic between the Christian story and its demands, quite similar to that found in the Old Testament. In Jewish tradition, the Torah contained two elements, the *haggadah* (narrative) and the *halakah* (commands). The Torah, on the one hand, included the rehearsal of the mighty acts of God, essential to the identity of Israel. On the other hand, woven into this narrative rehearsal was a call to a way of life. The narrative included the interpretation, that is, the specific implications of the mighty acts. The *act* and the *interpretation of the act* belonged together. The narrative dimension answered the question of identity, "Who are we?" The legal dimension containing commandments and instructions answered the question, "What are we to do?" The Torah did not emphasize one over the other but contained a combination of both. Commands and laws were integrated within the story.

---

[14] Ibid.

Paul integrates these two dimensions of the Torah into his letter to the Romans to offer guidelines in forming a dynamic community of faith. As Willi Marxsen astutely observes, "The Pauline imperatives are not intended just to invite people to act: they are addressed to *changed* people. Therefore they do not simply presuppose a 'known' indicative; they presuppose an indicative that has *affected* people."[15] James Walters maintains that the paradigm is more than the imperative (human responsibility) simply following the indicative (God's actions), leaving the impression that salvation is a fifty-fifty deal between God and humans. Rather, the proper relationship between the indicative and the imperative is stated more accurately in the phrase Walters uses, "become what God is continuing to make you."[16]

It is significant that the momentum of Romans, as well as most of Paul's letters, moves toward the question of how to live. So the paraenetic or exhortation section is not an appendix tacked on at the end because of the delay of the parousia. Rather it is the apex of Paul's correspondence to the church in Rome.[17]

---

[15] Willi Marxsen, *New Testament Foundations for Christian Ethics* (Minneapolis: Fortress, 1993), 187.

[16] See Walters, chapter one. For further development of the relationship between the indicative and imperative in Paul, see Michael Parsons, "Being Precedes Act," 217-32.

[17] Paraenetic material was frequently offered at transitional moments in life when communities were most vulnerable and most receptive to instruction. The precepts in Romans 12-15 appear to be offered at just such a time. They serve as moral guidelines for Jews and Gentiles as Jewish Christians make their way back into the church in Rome. See Leo Perdue, "The Social Character of Paraenesis and Paraenetic Literature," *Semeia*, 50 (1990), 27.

## *The Theological Content of Paul's Moral Vision*

Embedded within the overarching indicative/imperative paradigm are specific theological themes that shape Paul's ethic. Among them include the themes of community, new creation, the cross, and law. The first two deal with the *context* of moral instruction, the last two with its *content*. These themes reveal the moral vision Paul proclaims in the letter to the Romans.

For Paul, the community serves as the context for nurturing ethical conduct. Paul addresses the community, not the individual. In Romans, as well as in some of his other letters, Paul's primary focus is not the formation of the individual but "the corporate obedience of the church."[18] Romans 12:1-2 contains an example of this emphasis on community. Here Paul describes the church as "a living sacrifice." He calls on Christians in Rome to present their "bodies" (plural) as a collective "sacrifice" (singular) "holy and acceptable to God, which is your (plural) spiritual worship."

This reading stands in stark contrast to the way readers usually interpret the text, which understands it as an address to the individual Christian. But the *corporate* body is the focus of Paul's ethic. He continues in chapter 12 to describe how the one body is composed of diverse members (vv. 3-8). In Romans 15:14-19 Paul speaks of "the offering of the Gentiles," an image that also describes the corporate sacrifice of the body (15:16).

God saves and transforms individuals, yes, but in community. Paul directs his moral mandate to the

---

[18] Hays, 196.

church. He calls the faith community to embody an alternative lifestyle that emulates God's redemptive scheme at work in the world. Thus the well-being of the community always takes precedence over the rights of the individual.[19]

That is why Paul issues the following exhortation to the Gentiles in Rome: "We who are strong ought to put up with the failings of the weak, and not to please ourselves. Each of us must please our neighbor for the good purpose of building up the neighbor. For Christ did not please himself; but, as it is written, 'The insults of those who insult you have fallen on me'" (15:1-3).[20] That is why Paul himself gave up the desire to go on and be with the Lord—in order to stay and serve the church (Phil 1:21-25). Community has primacy over individuality because the faith community provides the matrix for nurturing individuals who live in the tension between the now-but-not-yet times.

While the community provides the supportive context for moral instruction, the community fulfills this role within a time-bounded context between the resurrection of Christ and his return. That is, moral development takes place in the now-but-not-yet times. This state is best captured in the theme of new creation, which also informs Paul's ethic. As new creation the church possesses the power of the Holy Spirit in the midst of a fallen world. The gravitational forces, however, from both worlds pull at the life of the faith community. This tension between the now and the not-yet leads neither to

---

[19] J. Paul Sampley, *Walking Between the Times: Paul's Moral Reasoning* (Minneapolis: Fortress, 1991), 42.

[20] All Scripture quotes come from the *New Revised Standard Version*, 3rd ed. (Oxford: Oxford University Press, 2001).

moral passivism nor to moral fanaticism but motivates the church to love and good works.[21] For example, Romans 5 envisions this in-between time where glory and suffering, life and death, righteousness and unrighteousness intermingle.[22] In this state, Christians experience freedom from the power of the flesh (8:1-17a). But at the same time they suffer (8:17b-25). This in-betweenness heightens the call for ethical conduct because God is at work continuing to shape us into his likeness.

In the now-but-not-yet state, the power of fleshly desires continues to invade the body. God does not, however, leave the community to its own devices. Paul's agonizing struggle with bondage to the flesh in Romans 7 is countered with the liberation he also experiences in Romans 8. This is the tension of the in-between state of the Christian life (7:24-25; 8:10). What makes the transition possible is the power of God's Spirit. The Spirit of God enables the Christian body to walk in a way that it otherwise could not walk, giving it strength to express full obedience to God. Fulfilling the law is not beyond the ability of God's people (Deut 30:11-14). Thus the church is expected to fulfill the law of Christ summed up by Paul in the practice of love.[23] Moral living means obedience to God's will.[24] God provides moral leadership through the power of the Holy Spirit for the between times (Rom 8:14).

The *context* of moral instruction takes place in the community which lives in the between times. Within this

---

[21] Hays, *Moral Vision*, 21.

[22] See Stephen Farris in chapter four.

[23] Rom 8:4; 13:8-10.

[24] Rom 1:5; 2:13; 6:16-18; 15:18.

context Paul strives to shape Christians into a unique body informed by the cross and by the law or Scripture. These two sources form the *content* of Paul's ethic.

In Romans, Jesus' death on the cross is the model for how the community lives faithfully before God. Paul admonishes the church to imitate Christ. In matters of conduct, decisions flow from Jesus' self-giving act at Calvary. The cross demonstrates God's righteousness and love (Rom 3:24-26; 5:8). Thus, the cross becomes a symbol of Christian conduct analogous to the self-sacrificial act of Christ.[25]   So in Romans 15 Paul says that the death of Christ constrains certain types of behavior (15:1-3, 7). Just as Christ suffered for others, especially the weak and helpless, so those who are strong ought to bear the burdens of the weak (Rom 14:15). Jewish and Gentile congregations must incarnate the cross in their own lives as they relate to one another: "For Christ did not please himself; but, as it is written, 'The insults of those who insult you have fallen on me'" (15:3). Conformity to Christ's sacrificial death stands in the background of Paul's vision of the moral life (see Rom 6:1-14; 8:17, 29-30; 15:1-7).

As important as the cross is for Paul, the law in Romans, that is the Old Testament Scripture, plays an even larger role in informing his ethics. In fact, in Romans, Paul seldom appeals to the cross as the motivation for ethical living. Paul's mention of the cross usually comes in the context of his discussion of salvation, not in his discussion of ethics.[26]   Contrary to popular theological belief, the cross does not stand central in

---

[25] Hays, 28.

[26] see Rom 3.

Paul's ethic. So for preachers to appreciate Paul's perspective on ethics, they must understand the role Scripture plays in his scheme.

In Romans, Paul most often appeals to Scripture as the basis for an ethical lifestyle. For example, in Romans 12, as Paul admonishes Jews and Gentiles to love one another, and even their enemies, he appeals to them not on the grounds of the cross but on the basis of Scripture.[27] Why are they not to repay evil for evil? Because Deuteronomy 32:35 assures believers that "Vengeance is mine, I will repay, says the Lord" (Rom 12:19). They are also not to seek revenge because of the admonition of the sages in Proverbs 25:21-22: "If your enemies are hungry, feed them; if they are thirsty, give them something to drink; for by doing this you will heap burning coals on their heads" (Rom 12:20). For Paul, Scripture carries its own authority: it shapes his moral vision.[28]

Paul bases the entire Gospel message he proclaims in Romans on the text from Habakkuk 2:4, "The one who is righteous will live by faith" (Rom 1:17). Out of this overarching framework of Scripture flows Paul's ethical mandates. He expects Jews, as well as Gentiles, to honor the law (3:29-31). It is the law that discloses God's will (Rom 7:12). So Paul tells Jews and Gentiles "whatever was written in former days was written for our instruction, so that by steadfastness and by the encouragement of the Scriptures we might have hope"

---

[27] Thanks to my colleague Richard Oster for bringing this, as well as other insights, to my attention.

[28] For a more detailed development of Paul's use of Scripture, see Richard B. Hays, "The Role of Scripture in Paul's Ethics," in *Theology & Ethics in Paul and His Interpreters*, eds. Eugene H. Lovering, Jr. and Jerry L. Sumney (Nashville: Abingdon Press, 1996), 30-47.

(Rom 15:4). Paul maintains that Scripture was written for moral instruction and encouragement.

Paul demonstrates this by the use of frequent allusions, images, and direct quotations from the Old Testament.[29] His opening list of vices in Romans 1:18-23 alludes to Scripture (Ps 106:20; Jer 2:11; see also Wisdom of Solomon 12:23-14:31). In addition, Scripture witnesses to the unquenchable appetite humans have for sin. In 3:10-18, Paul strings together a series of texts from the Old Testament that describe the moral depravity of all humanity, even to every part of the body from the eyes to the feet. Paul weaves these texts together from a variety of sources: Psalms (14:1-2; 53:1-2; 5:9; 140:3), Proverbs (1:16), and Isaiah (59:7-8).

Paul summarizes the essence of the law in 13:8-10 when he quotes a portion of the Ten Commandments from Exodus 20:13-17 and Deuteronomy 5:17-21: "You shall not commit adultery; You shall not murder; You shall not steal; You shall not covet." He then cites Leviticus 19:18 as the Scripture that encapsulates the essence of the law: "Love your neighbor as yourself" (13:9). Upon the basis of this Scripture Jews and Gentiles must relate to one another in love. Paul echoes the appeal to this text later in the letter when he says to the community: "Each of us must please our neighbor for the good purpose of building up the neighbor" (15:2).

One point, however, needs clarification. Paul does not view the law as rigid or inflexible. Scripture is not a rulebook. It is founded upon the principle of love. Certain cultic or ceremonial requirements of the law are not necessarily binding (Rom 14:1-4, 5). He must

---

[29] James Walters noted that Romans 1-4 and 9-11 contain fifty-three quotations from Israel's Scripture. See chapter one of this book.

remind the Jews that true circumcision is not "something external and physical..." (Rom 2:29). Recalling Deuteronomy 30:6, Paul maintains that "real circumcision is a matter of the heart—it is spiritual and not literal" (Rom 2:29). For Paul, Scripture teaches that understanding one's moral responsibility is a matter of being "transformed by the renewing of your minds" so that one learns to discern the will of God (Rom 12:2). Christians follow the law, not by practicing blind obedience, but by practicing spiritual discernment. Repeatedly Paul appeals to Scripture as the source that shapes the way Christians conduct themselves in the now-but-not-yet times.

These theological themes of community, new creation, the cross, and law, serve as the matrix of Paul's ethic. They provide the basis for evaluating any educational approach (whether religious or secular) that the church might wish to integrate into its teaching and preaching agenda. And they inform the message that the preacher as moral theologian proclaims. Paul's ethic is a community ethic. It is for the formation of a corporate identity. Any proclamation of a Christian ethic today must begin at this source. Any critique of a contemporary ethical system must use Paul as a paradigm.

## A Critique of the Contemporary Character Education Movement in Public Education

Over the past fifteen years a trend, generically referred to as the character education movement,[30] has gained significant momentum. The movement asserts

---

[30] Sometimes referred to as the Neoclassic Movement.

that one can identify and teach universal values to individuals. A number of influential people and organizations serve as spokespersons for the movement, including William Bennett, Gary Bauer, and organizations like the Character Counts! Coalition. Sympathetic with the movement is Stephen Covey, whose writings convey a strong sense of moral directives. Covey places the issue of character at the center of his formula for those who strive to be successful in whatever they do.[31] Representing evangelical Christianity, James Dobson lauds the efforts of these neoclassicists.

The character education movement speaks of "fixed" or "core" values, which are distilled from the consensus of the ages, including the great literature of western civilization. Proponents of this movement believe that values are objective. So one of their tasks is to identify the basic values they believe all major cultures and world religions share, such as courage, conviction, generosity, kindness, and honesty.[32] For example, the Character Counts! Coalition came together in Aspen, Colorado in 1992 to identify the core values that "transcend cultural, religious, and socio-economic differences."[33] The Coalition identified seven universal values: "respect, responsibility, trustworthiness, justice and fairness, caring, civic virtue, and citizenship."[34] Others, such as William Bennett in his *Book of Virtues*, rely on the great literature

---

[31] See for example *The 7 Habits of Highly Effective People* (New York: Simon & Schuster, 1989). See also, Stephen R. Covey, A. Roger Merrill, and Rebecca R. Merrill, *First Things First* (New York: Simon & Schuster, 1994).

[32] Bonnidell Clouse, *Teaching for Moral Growth: A Guide for the Christian Community Teachers, Parents, and Pastors* (Wheaton: BridgePoint, 1993), 63.

[33] Hunter, 117.

[34] Ibid.

of the past in western civilization from which to glean core values.[35]

This movement has implemented programs in thousands of public schools across the land.[36] Through a process of subtle enculturation, many evangelicals and mainline churches, as well, appear to have assimilated its writing and rhetoric via the world of psychology.[37] So how might Paul, as moral theologian, critique this movement?

On the one hand, the moral qualities that the movement identifies as "core values" resonate with Scripture and with Paul's teaching. Paul exhorts the church at Philippi, on one occasion, to dwell on whatever is true, honorable, just, pure, pleasing, and commendable (Phil 4:8). Not only would such a list receive approval by the character education movement today, the list also resembles those created by the Greek philosophers of Paul's day. Paul's paraenetic sections

[35] William Bennett, *The Book of Virtues* (New York: Simon & Schuster, 1993), 9, 15.

[36] Hunter identifies a number of states in the decade of the last century that enacted laws requiring school systems to develop programs for character education, 117-21. Examples of curricula used in the public schools include the following: Jeri A. Carroll, Marsha A. Gladhart, and Dixie L. Petersen, *Character Building: Literature-Based Theme Units* (Carthage, IL: Teaching & Learning Company, 1997); Barbara Allman, *Developing Character When It Counts: A Program for Teaching Character in the Classroom* (Torrance, CA: Frank Schaffer Publications, 1999); Sara Freeman, *Spotlight on Character: Plays That Show Character Counts!* (Torrance, CA: Frank Schaffer Publications, 1999).

[37] Hunter documents the way in which many evangelical writers (e.g., James Dobson, Kenneth Erickson, Charles Gerber, and Nell Mohney) have inculcated psychology and the therapeutic culture into their writings. Hunter also documents how a focus on self-esteem and the therapeutic mindset influences written material published by various Protestant groups such as the United Church of Christ, the United Methodist church, and some mainline Presbyterian churches. Two religious groups who seem to be less influenced by the therapeutic culture are Catholicism and Judaism. See Hunter, 129-45.

(e.g., Rom 12-15) teach values that both his culture and ours would herald as honorable. As Abraham Malherbe observes: "Paraenesis was a style of exhortation used to influence conduct rather than teach something new. It was, accordingly, used widely by moral philosophers who sought to modify the conduct of their audiences. Paraenesis stressed what was traditional, self-evidently good, and generally applicable."[38] In a similar manner, many of the values the character education movement identifies as core echo those identified by Paul.

On the other hand, two interrelated qualities that serve as the understructure to contemporary moral education programs stand in opposition to a Pauline ethic. For one, these programs strive for inclusiveness. They seek to find the values that every belief system can accept. They do so through the discipline of psychology or through the consensus of great western literature and anthropology. The goal is to discover values that generate no friction, those upon which everyone can agree. The result is that contemporary moral education ends up creating a system of generic values.[39]

One of the greatest fears of moral educators today is that they will be accused of indoctrinating students into a particular religious faith—the unpardonable sin. In response to a question about the place of religious and moral values in public schools, William Bennett voiced the predominant feeling of the majority of contemporary moral educators when he said, "values can and should be taught in schools...without fear of accusations of

---

[38] Abraham J. Malherbe, "Paul: Hellenistic Philosopher or Christian Pastor?" *American Theological Library Association Proceedings* 39 (June 1985), 92-93.

[39] Hunter, 215.

proselytizing."[40] This approach results in domesticating morals. Character education advocates do not want to offend anyone, while at the same time they strive to satisfy as many as possible.

Furthermore, the purpose of contemporary moral education is to enable individuals to have confidence in themselves, to improve physical, emotional, and mental health. Over the past fifty years, the primary reason given for instruction in ethical behavior focuses on the need to build self-esteem in children.[41] This is true even among Christian evangelicals, some of whom champion the recent revival in character education in this country. According to James Dobson in *Preparing for Adolescence*, the reason for understanding our sexual feelings and for abstaining from sexual activity is grounded in a concern for improving self-esteem.[42]

The goal of moral education, therefore, is for individuals to feel good about themselves, gain confidence, and reach their full potential. The focus begins and ends with the individual. There is nothing larger than the individual's story. In tracing the history of moral education in this country, Hunter concludes, "there has been a transformation in the *purpose of moral education* itself— from mastery over the soul in service to God and neighbor, to the training of character to serve

---

[40] Quoted in an interview with Michael Cromartie, "Virtue Man," *Christianity Today*, 37 no. 10 (September 1993), 33.

[41] Hunter, 98.

[42] James Dobson, *Preparing for Adolescence* (Ventura, CA: Regal Books, 1989). Whereas Dobson is quite concerned with Christian morality, in the end the purpose is primarily for the development of a healthy self-esteem and not for bringing glory to God. Self-esteem is the first chapter in the book. Other chapters follow suit in dealing with different emotions.

the needs of civic life, to the cultivation of personality toward the end of well-being."[43]

In contrast, Paul understands ethics in the larger context of the story of what God is doing in this world and in particular what he is doing in the now-but-not-yet times. Christians are a part of God's story in bringing *all* people into relationship with him. One cannot separate moral responsibility from the redemptive work of God. The contemporary movement in moral education fails because the desire for inclusiveness begins and ends with a focus on the individual and on self-esteem.

Inclusiveness results in an emphasis on the individual, which ultimately leads to the second and interrelated characteristic underlying the popular moral movement: a lack of community. Moral instruction is not integrated into the surrounding culture as a way of life. The outcry today by politicians and various institutions is, "We need more moral education in order to better our culture." But in reality, the moral education movement, like the church, simply *reflects* the larger American culture rather than offering an alternative.

Individuals learn values by being a part of a purpose larger than any single person. Christians learn morals through a faith community that instructs, models, mentors, and practices Christian values. We learn values by being a part of a supportive community environment which serves and worships together, holding its members accountable. Moral education does not take place in a vacuum. It is a natural part of the environment.

When Paul speaks of moral conduct, he refers to a specific Christian context that takes place in the between times. The qualities he calls on Christians to emulate are

---

[43] Hunter, 147.

imbedded in Scripture, as well as the story of the cross. When a pluralistic culture strives to include more and more moral diversity, morals become detached from their moorings. No ground of authority exists, no context, no community. Morals are decontextualized, detached from the traditions, rituals, liturgy, and Scriptures of the community. They become free-floating, hollow, and ultimately vacuous. The imperative is stripped from the indicative. Such values no longer possess authority and individuals no longer possess the resources for inculcating them.

Both the concern for inclusiveness and the lack of community work against the ability of the moral education movement to make a difference in the society at large. The movement has little sense of the now-but-not-yet context, which drives Christian conduct. And though it echoes Christian values, the movement possesses little understanding of the source of those values as found in Scripture and the cross.

The tragedy is that the Christian church often merely mirrors the surrounding culture rather than offering itself as an alternative community. In order to address the needs of the individual, churches adopt a therapeutic mindset, which leads them to see their primary purpose as providing individuals relief from the anxieties of life. Many Christians now view their relationship with God as a way of enabling them to feel better about the decisions they make and about the lifestyle they choose to live. The church is rendered anemic in imparting guidance for making daily moral decisions about Christian conduct.

Preachers, in part, carry the liability for the moral anemia of the church. In the arena of ethics, their voices

remain amazingly mute.  Preachers place themselves on
the sidelines simply by conceding to the cultural norms of
the day, rather than offering a counter image informed by
Scripture.  They often find themselves intimidated by the
"experts" and acquiesce to *their* moral agenda.

## *The Preacher as Moral Theologian: A Vision of God's Kingdom*

Preachers bear the responsibility of offering a
counter-cultural voice.  The task of preaching involves
interpreting, critiquing, and shaping a church made up of
diverse individuals into a community that displays
Christian moral conduct.  The preacher functions
as moral theologian.  What role do sermons play in
nurturing moral vision and skills in the faith community?
In light of Paul's approach, I would like to offer some
preaching suggestions for moral formation that take
preachers off the sidelines and enable them to proclaim a
clear vision.

First, as moral theologians, preachers must preach
primarily for community formation and secondarily to
the individual.  Christian ethics are formed in the context
of the faith community.  As Sally Brown puts it,
"Preaching on ethics means above all the proclamation of
the taking-form of Jesus Christ in the church."[44]
Becoming a Christian is a process of enculturation within
a particular community.  One learns the biblical language,
skills, habits, traditions, and behaviors by which the
community operates.

[44] Sally Brown, "Rethinking the Moral-Theological Tasks of Peaching: The
Case for Reviving the Conversation between Homiletics and Christian
Ethics," Academy of Homiletics papers (Dallas: December, 2000), 213.

In other words, Christians learn morals by being immersed in the Christian culture, listening, imitating, developing, and growing. The Christian story shapes the entirety of thought and life. Learning to be a Christian is a communal journey, not an individual experiential event. This does not mean that preaching ignores the individual and particular individual problems, but rather it views the individual within the context of the *ecclesia*. In this communal context, preaching listens to Scripture, critiques contemporary culture, and offers an alternative community.

One important qualification needs mentioning at this point. Preachers must understand the context and limitations of the sermon. On its own, the sermon cannot create moral communities. Listening exclusively to sermons does not form character.[45] We must understand the sermon's function in the larger context of body life. Apart from a community that is worshipping, studying Scripture, serving others, and striving to live faithfully for God, it is doubtful that preaching will make much difference. Preaching has its greatest effect in the context of a faithful, worshipping community.[46]

Second, preachers must engage the conversation of ethics at the level of a *moral vision for the church* rather than at the level of deliberation over specific moral issues. Preachers who come from an issue-centered paradigm focus on the heated ethical quandaries of the day, such as abortion, homosexuality, gambling, capital punishment, and others that often occupy the headlines of the evening

[45] Charles Campbell, "More Than Quandaries: Character Ethics and Preaching," *Journal for Preachers* 16 no 4 (1993) : 34.

[46] This is the thesis of Charles Rice in his book, *The Embodied Word: Preaching as Art and Liturgy* (Minneapolis: Fortress, 1991).

news. Preaching ethics is viewed as synonymous with knowing the particular stand Christians should take on the moral dilemmas of the day. When preachers address the difficult moral dilemmas, some believe they lead the congregation to moral responsibility.

It is not that preachers do not address specific moral issues. But these issues cannot be addressed apart from who we are as Christians. If Christians do not possess a clear focus of identity, then they cannot deal responsibly with the major moral quandaries of the day. Stanley Hauerwas observes, "...what is at stake in most of our decisions is not the act itself, but the kind of persons we will be...."[47] In other words, morality is not limited to moments in life that call on one to make a difficult decision. Instead, morality incorporates the whole of life. Morality includes the mundane affairs of life, as well as the tough decisions one faces, precisely Paul's point in Romans 13:8-10. Here Paul lists specific moral issues: do not commit adultery, do not murder, do not steal, and do not covet. But these imperatives flow out of the deeper base of one's character. Thus Paul says that all of these specific commands derive from the ethical responsibility to "Love your neighbor as yourself" (Lev 19:18). Then he adds, "Love does no wrong to a neighbor; therefore, love is the fulfilling of the law" (13:10). The character of the person in community remains central to Paul's ethic. One's character determines how one makes difficult ethical decisions.

"Character ethics" means that preaching encompasses a broader responsibility than just an occasional sermon on a moral dilemma. If the purpose of preaching is to

---

[47] Stanley Hauerwas, *Character and the Christian Life: A Study in Theological Ethics* (San Antonio: Trinity University Press, 1975), 7-8.

build up the body, then every sermon will in essence be an ethical sermon, even though, as Campbell observes, the sermon "may not seem to be focused directly on moral concerns."[48] The important question for preachers becomes this: Into what shape do we want to mold the body?

Paul Lehmann gets to the heart of the task when he says that the starting point for Christian ethics is the nature of the body of Christ. The aim of Christian ethics is "the socialization of humanity into its moral vision by incorporation into the social reality of the *koinonia*...the moral life is fundamentally context-specific and socially constructed."[49] In Romans, Paul deals with the problem between Jews and Gentiles by addressing the issue of character and what kind of people the church ought to be.

A third suggestion for preaching moral formation is to remember that Paul calls on the church at Rome to live within the world of Scripture. For him it is Scripture that shapes the moral identity of the faith community. For preachers to follow Paul's lead means that we immerse ourselves in the language and thought of Scripture. It means that the Old Testament serves as a foundation of our ethic, as it did for Paul (Rom 15:4). We live and breathe its thought-world. As Mark Love affirms in chapter 5, preachers "must dwell in the living pages of Scripture." Our preaching will manifest this Scripture-informed quality consistently from week to week as we proclaim the divine word.[50] When that word is faithfully

---

[48] Campbell, 33.

[49] Quoted by Sally Brown, 213.

[50] The sermons in Part 2 stand as representatives of this quality.

proclaimed, the lives of people change. For Paul, ethics is a matter of hearing and responding to God's word.

Finally, preachers proclaim the larger vision of what the community is about during the between times. The development of moral character takes place in the context of a faith community and in the presence of a goal that is greater than any one individual. If the primary goal of moral development is simply to feel better as a person, or if it is to gain self-esteem, then values will not have deep roots. Values are formed within faith communities that understand themselves as part of a larger story: the story of God working in the lives of his people to bring them into relationship with him.

Paul called on the house churches in Rome to see themselves as part of a story that had its origins in a remote time and place in Palestine in an itinerant teacher known as Jesus Christ. This was an especially tall order for Roman citizens steeped in all the world philosophies of the day. Paul calls them, however, to a different story founded in Scripture and incarnated in Christ. This story was much bigger and more dynamic than the Greco-Roman stories on which they cut their teeth. This gospel story must now shape their lives.

In preaching for moral character, preachers never stray far from the gospel story that shapes our lives. William Willimon, in one of his sermons at Duke University Chapel, tells of the following experience, which I paraphrase:

A few years ago a recruiter from the Teach America Program visited the university. Teach America is an organization which recruits this nation's best college and university students to teach in the most impossible situations in our country.

This recruiter from Teach America looked out on a crowd of Duke students. She began by saying, "I can tell by looking at you that I have probably come to the wrong place. Somebody told me this was a BMW campus and I can believe it by looking at you. Why would you even be on this campus if you were not successful, if you were not going on to successful careers on Madison Avenue or Wall Street?

"And yet here I stand, hoping to talk one of you into giving away your life in the toughest job you will ever have. I am looking for people to go into the hollows of West Virginia, the deltas of Mississippi, into the ghettos of south Los Angeles and teach in some of the most difficult schools in the world. Last year, two of our teachers were killed while on the job.

"But I can tell, just by looking at you, that none of you are interested in that. So go on to law school, go on to Madison Avenue, find a place with a major accounting firm or whatever successful career you are planning on doing.

"But if by chance, some of you just happen to be interested, I've got these brochures here for you that describe what Teach America is about....Meeting's over."

With that, the whole group stood up, pushed into the aisles, shoved each other aside, ran down to the front, and fought over the brochures! Why?

We want to be a part of something greater than our own personal success or happiness or achieving self-esteem. We want to be a part of a larger mission. James Hunter describes the context in which character is developed in this way:

> It will be found...within families and communities that still, somehow, embody a moral vision....In such settings people will not merely acquire techniques of moral improvement but rather find themselves encompassed within a story that defines their own purposes within a shared destiny, one that points toward aims that are higher and greater than themselves.[51]

Moral character can only develop in the context of a faith community shaped by the word of Scripture and in the presence of a goal greater than any single person. The power of preaching resides in giving Christians a glimpse of the larger story of which we are a part. We are part of a story of an inscrutable God who created the world and whose thoughts and ways are far beyond human understanding; from him, through him, and to him all creation exists (Rom 11:33-36). We are part of a story of a God who sent his only Son to reconcile all humanity to himself. When we get caught up in that story, moral values assume a whole new meaning and dimension. Preaching challenges Christians to see themselves as a part of this grand vision. Preaching reminds the church that the task of moral development is not about "me." It is about God's kingdom coming into a fallen world.[52]

---

[51] Hunter, 227.

[52] See Dave Bland, "The Church's Role in the Development of Moral Character," *Mid-South Christian Banner*, Vol. 5, no. 6 (August, 2001), 9.

# 4

# *When in Romans:*
## Preaching from the Fifth Chapter of Romans
### Stephen Farris

I have argued elsewhere[1] that preachers may move between the world of the text and the world of the listener by way of analogy. Once an analogy or a small series of analogies between those worlds is identified, it is relatively easy, or at least possible, to "grow" a sermon. Most preachers already think in an analogical fashion but do so unconsciously and unsystematically. A more careful and reflective form of analogical thinking can present considerable advantages to us, however. It demands that we think carefully and faithfully about both the world of the biblical text and the world in which we live, a necessity for preaching that intends to be both faithful and relevant. It can enable us to perceive connections between the two and, in some cases, may even suggest a structure for the sermon itself. Such thinking is not, however, always easy. In fact, as we shall see, Romans is one of the most difficult books of the Bible from which to practice this kind of analogical thinking.

This essay is not an exercise in New Testament studies but in homiletics. To be more precise, it is an exercise in analogical thinking for homiletical purposes.

---

[1] Stephen Farris, *Preaching That Matters: The Bible and Our Lives* (Louisville: Westminster John Knox Press, 1998).

As an exercise in homiletics, this essay will of necessity not only reflect on the biblical text but will also reflect on what the text shows us about our society. The biblical scholar primarily examines the text. The preacher joins in that study but then *uses* the text to examine the contemporary world to bear witness to the presence of God in our world. The preacher's Bible may be understood under two optical images: as a mirror which shows us our true selves and as a lens through which we may look more clearly at the world around us. Therefore, I conceive of my task in this essay in this way: to show how a preacher may reflect analogically on a preaching text in Romans and to use that text to speak on and to our present world.

The text I shall use in this manner is Romans 5:1-11. That choice is not self-evident and requires some defense. Of all the specifically homiletical tasks, the determination of the limits of the preaching text is one of the most significant for interpretation. The meaning of a text can be radically altered for listeners by the choice of limits. Some choice is, however, necessary. The most common complaint I hear from people in the church about student preachers is some version of "Why do they think they have to tell us everything they know in one sermon?" Nor can it be said that this is a fault of beginning students only. Veteran preachers may also be tempted to cram too much into one sermon. That temptation may be almost overwhelming with a text as theologically rich as Romans 5. It is usually wiser, however, to say a few things *well* rather than many things poorly! The three key words in sermon composition may be "focus, focus, and focus."[2] To that end, a more manageable unit of thought must be chosen.

Cutting a text into units is never as easy with Paul as it is with other parts of Scripture. Paul frequently summarizes what he has just said and anticipates what he is about to say in a linking passage that could be assigned either to what comes before or to what comes after. It may be that an entire epistle of Paul was read aloud when it arrived at its destination. This is no longer practicable except with respect to the little letter to Philemon. The contemporary preacher is normally required to begin reading at some particular point and to stop at some other, preferably not too distant, point. In our case, it appears possible to divide this chapter into two readings, Romans 5:1-11 and 12-21. In the Revised Common Lectionary, the former unit is read on Lent 3, Year A.[3]

Romans 5:1 is a point at which Paul recapitulates in a phrase all that has gone before. Many commentators consider that it begins not just a unit of thought but a

---

[2] This is, in fact, a preacher's overstatement for effect. Other words such as faithfulness, obviously also matter. There are, however, certain trends in preaching that make focus a greater concern than in the past. Older-style preaching tended to abstract sentences or even phrases from the pericope to serve as texts: "For God So Loved," or "And After that the Judgement." More recent preaching has tended to work with larger units of thought: pericopes as a whole or even wider cycles within a book. With respect to the latter style of preaching, see Robert Reid, *Preaching Mark* (St. Louis: Chalice, 1999). Such sermons may well deal more appropriately with the text in its proper context— but the danger of loss of focus is clearly multiplied.

[3] Shorter units of thought might even be possible. Romans 5:1-5 is read on Trinity Sunday in year C. Romans 5:1-8 is read on the sixth Sunday after Pentecost in year A. (This is a season in which Romans is read in a semi-continuous fashion in the Lectionary.) The latter division does not seem an exegetically responsible choice. It breaks Paul's thought halfway through a "from the lesser to the greater" argument. The chosen reading leaves out the "more."

major section of the Epistle as a whole.[4] In verse 12, Paul turns to a typological comparison of Christ and Adam that is related to, but distinct from, the earlier part of the chapter. To concentrate on Romans 5:1-11 appears to be a responsible choice both for a sermon and for an essay on preaching from Romans.

It is not my intention, however, to provide here an exegesis even for this shorter unit of thought. There are, after all, more than enough good commentaries on the letter to the Romans. Romans is to the expert on Paul what Beethoven's Ninth Symphony is to conductors; the very best all try their hand at it. Nor shall I review the literature on this text. Rather, I shall assume in the reader some degree of familiarity with the text and specifically mention exegetical issues only as they arise in the course of our analogical reflection. A warning must be sounded here, however. The first step in effective biblical preaching, a thorough exegesis of the text, may not be skipped in the actual preparation of a sermon. Without thorough exegesis, whatever analogy we perceive may well be unsound on its biblical side.[5]

In actual practice, we begin to perceive analogies in the course of the exegesis itself. But, for the sake of the

---

[4] As an example of contrasting treatments of the division of the text, compare two of the best-known commentaries on Romans, those of Paul Achtemeier and C. E. B. Cranfield. Paul Achtemeier notes that Paul develops themes from 4:23-25 in our text and therefore identifies the unit of thought as 4:23-5:11. (Paul Achtemeier, *Romans* [Atlanta: John Knox, 1985], 89-90). Cranfield, by contrast, considers 4:25 a "solemn formula" that concludes a major section of the work and notes various themes which bind our text to the succeeding four chapters. (C. E. B. Cranfield, *The Epistle to the Romans* vol. I [Edinburgh: T. & T. Clark, 1975], 252-54). It may be that this text functions as a hinge in the epistle as a whole. One may examine the hinge without determining whether it belongs to the door or the frame.

[5] I have outlined an exegetical method for the preacher in *Preaching that Matters*, 51-74.

exercise, let us assume that we have already completed an exegesis of the text. We may then begin our analogical thinking with a simple step:

1. *Identify the persons or groups in or behind the text.* We then ask a question:

2. *How we are like and unlike the persons or groups we have identified?* The first step is an easy task with respect to narratives. For example, it is easy to perceive and then to preach analogies between the "prodigal son" in Jesus' great parable and people in our world and between his far country and the various forms of lostness that we experience. It is even easier to see analogies between the older son in that great parable and those of us who have never strayed from the Father's house.[6] At first sight, it appears possible to think this way about Romans 5. In that chapter there are two implied stories, the story of Jesus Christ and, in the second half of the chapter, the story of Adam. We are linked to one or the other of these great stories. Paul believes, however, that we are linked in more than an analogical fashion to Jesus Christ. It is not simply that in some way we are, or can be, or even ought to be like Jesus, true though that may be. There is more than the popular acronym "WWJD" here. In Paul's view, we as members of the church are also members of Christ. This is an objective, indeed, a cosmic reality and not just a narrative one. We have been "in Adam" and are "in Christ," one of Paul's favorite phrases. Merely to draw an analogy between ourselves and Christ or between ourselves and Adam is to oversimplify Paul's thought.

It may also be possible, however, to seek an analogy between ourselves and the *people behind the text*

---

[6] For an analogical treatment of this parable and a sermon on it, see *Preaching that Matters*, 107-15 and 135-9.

rather than in the text. In other words, there may be an analogy in either a narrative or non-narrative text between ourselves and the people to whom the text is written.

Sometimes this kind of analogical thinking is also quite easy. As an idle fancy I have sometimes wondered what chair the Apostle Paul would hold in a contemporary theological seminary. He would certainly not teach homiletics; he might think it too much "lofty words of wisdom" (1 Cor 2:1). Nor, perhaps, would systematic theology be his chosen field. Old Testament interpretation would be a possibility, but I think he would find himself most at home as the professor of pastoral theology. Paul has a positive genius for understanding the specific problems of the churches he has founded in light of his fundamental theology. In most of his epistles Paul is addressing specific pastoral problems and when he does so he makes it easy for analogical preachers. Why? Because it is very likely that there are analogous problems in our world.

For example, Paul addresses the church in Corinth: "Now I appeal to you, brothers and sisters, by the name of our Lord Jesus Christ that all of you be in agreement and that there be no divisions among you...For it has been reported to me by Chloe's people that there are quarrels among you..." (1 Cor 1:10-11). There is trouble and division in the church. If we read a few verses more, we find that the trouble is about favorite preachers. If we read a few chapters farther still, we find that there are other troubles as well: troubles over sexual ethics, the person and work of the Holy Spirit, and speaking in tongues. The preacher who cannot name contemporary analogs to these troubles is several sopranos short of a full choir. Even where the problem is not all but repeated in our present experience, it is usually possible to discern *something* similar in our world. For example, there are no quarrels in our churches over meat offered to idols but Paul's principle of a liberty that refuses to abuse the tender consciences of the weak moves very nicely by way of analogy to a variety of perplexing issues today. I think you need some modern parallels here.. In short, pastoral problems make analogical preaching easy.

But Paul doesn't know the church in Rome, or at least he does not know it well. Paul does, however, appear to know a surprising number of church members there by name (Rom 16:1-16). As Fred Craddock once said, "I wonder if back then you could buy mailing lists."[7] Though some knowledge of difficulties in the church of Rome may lie behind his formulations, he does not explicitly and unambiguously address any pastoral problems they may have. A very bright student once said to me in class, "A lot of exegesis is like playing *Jeopardy*. It is trying to figure out the questions to which the text is the answer." Where there are problems, this particular "game" is easy. In this case, however, there is no charming host to tell us if our answers are correct. Our guesses remain just that—and it is unwise to base too much of our preaching on mere supposition.

Thus it may be best to confine ourselves in our preaching to that which seems certain, or at least very likely, from a close reading of the text as it stands. Paul is writing to the Romans to explain the gospel he preaches and to gain support from this influential church for his

---

[7] See his magnificent sermon, "When the Roll is Called Down Here." This sermon may be found in Mark Elliot, *Creative Styles of Preaching* (Louisville: Westminster/John Knox Press, 2000), 14-18.

future endeavors, most notably a proposed missionary journey to Spain. It is clear from Paul's other letters that he knows he is a controversial figure in early Christianity. It appears that he is aware that he must explain himself and his gospel to the church in Rome. As a result, the letter contains a detailed exposition of the gospel and the consequent responsibilities of the Christian that is as close to systematic theology as anything the greatest pastoral theologian of the first century would ever write. The letter does not, therefore, speak of the kind of specific pastoral challenges that make analogical preaching easier.[8] Nevertheless, the letter is written to a specific church and analogical thinking ought to be possible, though admittedly difficult, with respect to the Epistle to the Romans.

There are certain similarities between ourselves and the church in Rome. In the first place we, like them, are Christians, surely an obvious point, but equally surely, one that must not be ignored. Those who receive the letter are Christians already; Paul writes "to all God's beloved in Rome, to the called saints" (Rom 1:7, my translation). Paul does not have to start from scratch with these people. He can assume a certain basic familiarity with the gospel. They already know, though doubtless they do not fully understand, the implications of the claim that "at the right time Christ died for the ungodly." His strategy may be to remind them of what they already know, rather than to inform them of something new. James Thompson has noted that this is

---

[8] It must be emphasized again that I am not claiming here that Paul has no knowledge whatever of the situation in the Roman church. Manifestly, however, this epistle lacks the very specific references to persons, issues, and even previous correspondence that we find in other epistles. It is those specific references to pastoral difficulties that make analogical preaching easy.

a typical part of Paul's strategy when writing to the churches in which he has preached.[9] It may likewise be a strategy he can employ with this church he does not yet know.

Much the same could be said of our listeners. They too are Christians and have some familiarity with the core of the gospel. Preaching in our churches can also take the form of reminding the listeners of what they already know. As we shall see, however, this familiarity with the core of the gospel ought not to be overestimated.

But, once again, Paul does not know this church and they do not know him. He comes to them as a stranger: perhaps, given his troubles with the Judaizers, as a slightly suspect stranger. Even more importantly, Paul cannot assume that they will fully understand the Gospel he preaches. That this is the case is indicated by the length of the epistle and the evident care with which it is written. It cannot be assumed that the Gospel as Paul preaches it will be well received in Rome. Nor can it be assumed that preaching Paul's Gospel will be well received by all our listeners today. Paul remains a stranger for us and his Gospel, too, will often seem foreign. There are at least currents in the church that suggest that Paul is a corrupter of the simple Gospel of Jesus, introducing dogma where once there was simple beauty. He may also be accused of sexism and of an unhealthy attitude to the body and its needs. At the very least, in an age that loves narrative, he is out of fashion.[10] It cannot be presumed

[9] James Thompson, *Preaching Like Paul: Homiletical Wisdom for Today* (Louisville: Westminster John Knox, 2001), 54-5. At this point, Thompson is speaking primarily of Paul's custom of reminding the churches of what they already know about Paul and his ministry with them. This strategy is even more obvious with respect to the work of Christ (145).

[10] Ibid, 14-16.

in many churches that a sermon on Paul will meet
unqualified approval.

We may also note that Paul is writing to an important
and influential church. They are inhabitants of Rome, the
capital of the world's sole remaining superpower.[11] They
may be small in number and scorned by the
influential,[12] but they are Romans! Let me assume here
that most readers of this essay will be Americans.
You and your listeners are citizens of the world's sole
remaining superpower. The extent to which the church
retains power and influence in this society is doubtful
and certainly the opinion molders of this society do
not always speak well of the church. But you, and they,
are Americans! As a Canadian, let me be the first to
acknowledge it—that's something special.

To this point we have discussed similarities that apply
when considering every text in the epistle. There are also

---

[11] It might be noted that one can describe the other side of the analogy,
that is, the world of the biblical text, in terms drawn from this side of the analogy, as in "the world's sole remaining superpower." This prepares the listeners to grasp the analogy. In fact, if this is done carefully enough, it is not necessary to draw the analogy explicitly to the listeners' attention.

[12] The "media" of the day did not think well of Christians. Here is what
the historian Tacitus said about the Christians in explaining why Nero chose
them as scapegoats for the great fire in Rome. That fire occurred ca. 62 AD,
a very short period after the writing of the epistle. "Consequently, to get rid
of the report, Nero fastened the guilt and inflicted the most exquisite tortures
on a class hated for their abominations, called Christians by the populace.
Christus, from whom the name had its origin, suffered the extreme penalty
during the reign of Tiberius at the hands of one of our procurators, Pontius
Pilatus, and a most mischievous superstition, thus checked for the moment,
again broke out not only in Judaea, the first source of the evil, but even in
Rome, where all things hideous and shameful from every part of the world
find their centre and become popular." This is the quotation as it appears at
www.classics.mit.edu/Tacitus/annals.html Book XV, translated by Alfred
John Church and William Jackson Brodribb.

differences between the Roman Christians and ourselves that could be raised in connection with every text in the epistle. To give but one example, American Christians live in a nation where much of the leadership of the state (including the equivalent of the emperor) is at least formally Christian, but the Romans lived in a situation where the authorities were indifferent and very soon would be hostile. There are, however, also differences that spring to mind from a consideration of this text in particular. One of those differences can profitably be explored here at some length as an example of the way such thinking can lead directly from the study to the pulpit.

Paul says that at the right time Christ died for us "while we were still weak" (Rom 5:6). In Christ, God has done for us what we were and are incapable of doing for ourselves. It is hard to say how readily the Roman Christians would have recognized themselves as weak. While Rome itself was immensely powerful, they as outsiders in their society might well have been ready to recognize their own weakness. At the very least, we can say that they took the trouble to preserve the epistle that contains these words. It would, however, certainly cut against the grain in our society to accept that we are weak. Such a recognition would demand that we acknowledge ourselves as helpless. "For while we were still weak at the right time Christ died for the ungodly..." is a hard sell in our time. Far more acceptable would be some version of the quintessential North American creed, "The Lord helps them that helps themselves." The difference may be put this way: the Romans were "weak" and may have realized it. We are also "weak" but will likely have a hard time believing it.

We are a society that believes fervently in self-help. We preachers may be tempted to preach self-help, probably because our society is in love with the idea. Think, for example, of myriad self-help books available today. If you read them,

> You're going to *Do Less and Have More* (in five easy steps), *Whip Your Career Into Submission* and *Organize Your House From the Inside Out.* After you *Heal From the Heart* and *Find Mr. Right,* you'll unravel the secret to *Hot Sex* and discover why you shouldn't *Sweat the Small Stuff in Love.* Then you'll *Make the Connection* to a better body (while writing it all down in your *Journal of Daily Renewal*), begin to *Eat Right for Your Type, Learn the Seven Habits of Highly Effective People* and *Retire Wealthy in the 21st Century.*[13]

These books sell considerably better than the proverbial hotcakes. A leader in the Canadian publishing industry puts it simply, "Self-help blows fiction out of the water."[14] That is a Canadian reality—but is it likely to be very different in the land of the free and the home of the Oprah?

It's quite possible to verify this interest in self-help writing. An interesting exercise to undertake and then describe in the pulpit is to look at cover articles in the magazine rack of the corner store. A huge percentage of the titles will have to do with self-help. Most of the titles

---

[13] Alexandra Gill, "Note to Self: Change Life Now." *The Toronto Globe and Mail,* January 1, 2000. (Note the date!)

[14] Alexandra Gill, "Note to Self: Change Life Now."

tell us how to get fit, lose weight, or earn more money. "Learn to be a more effective negotiator," they'll tell us. "Get the most out of your computer," or "Have a spring/summer/fall/winter makeover." My favorite title when I tried this exercise was, "Fifteen Ways to Fake Fabulous Skin!"

This kind of thinking is not foreign to our churches. On a church sign near my home appears a weekly "gospel." The sign recently read "Improvement begins with 'I' "! A society addicted to self-help remedies might not welcome a word that reminds us that Christ died for the helpless. Our core theology is often enshrined in our hymns and, in such a climate, we begin to change the words to hymns, not just to become inclusive but to reflect the gospel we live by. A hymnbook committee, left unnamed here to protect the guilty, once changed the words of a beloved children's hymn. No longer were we to sing:

"Jesus loves me this I know, for the Bible tells me
    so.
Little ones to him belong. We are weak but he is
    strong."

Now we were directed to sing:

"In his love we will be strong."

We then also ask: *Was the text a confirmation or a challenge to its first hearers?* The answer to this one is clear: this text is completely confirmation. It announces with great joy that "we have peace with God through our Lord Jesus Christ" (Rom 5:1). With the majority of commentators, I read the indicative rather than the subjunctive here. An early copyist, probably a preacher, wrote, "We should have peace with God!" It is not just ancient copyists who want to turn indicatives into subjunctives or even imperatives. We preachers often seem to suffer from a compulsion to tell people what to do. Paul doesn't do that here. He announces the good news and, if he resists our moralizing tendencies, so can we.

This leads naturally into the next questions:

*What Does the Text Do?*

*How Can the Sermon Appropriately Do the Same?*

There are instances in which a Christian sermon ought not to do the same as the scriptural text. A preacher today ought not, for example, long for the death of the children of our enemies: "Happy shall they be who take your little ones and dash them against the rock" (Ps 137:9).[15] There should be no such difficulty with our text, however! It states quite baldly that we have peace with God through Christ. It declares that this reality is so strong that we can even have joy in the midst of suffering. It declares that God has done all this through the death and resurrection of Jesus Christ. Surely a sermon ought appropriately to be able to do just that. The question, of course, is "How?"

What is happening here could be expressed in several ways. The preacher could use the language of purpose or meaning in life, for example. One might say that Christians may find the meaning of their lives in a relationship with God, created and shaped by the death

---

[15] The original version of this paper was written well before the terrorist outrages of September 11, 2001. Those terrible events certainly help us to understand the anger and despair that led the exiles in Babylon to say such horrible words. I maintain most firmly, however, that no follower of the one who said "Father, forgive them" from the cross may rightly wish for the death of the children of the enemy. Specifically, no Christian preacher ought, on the basis of this text, long for the death of the children of Afghanistan. In short, we cannot rightly do what this text does. With respect to the difficulties of preaching this text, see *Preaching that Matters*, 82-88 and 105-07.

and resurrection of Jesus Christ. It seems to me more faithful to the text, however, to speak first of relationship with God and a consequent new identity.[16] (In the second half of the chapter, Paul clearly uses "identity" language. We are in Adam or we are in Christ.) Here Paul speaks of our relationship with God. "We are justified by faith…we have peace with God…the grace in which we stand, we have now received reconciliation." As a result of God's gracious initiative, we have a new status before God. This status in relationship adds up to our Christian identity.

We can add to this insight some of the material we have already covered. Paul is writing to the Romans, inviting them to find their identity not in their status in the empire but in their status before God. The most important thing about the Romans is not that they are inhabitants, whether great or small, of the greatest and most influential city of earth, but that they have peace with God through the Lord Jesus Christ. The most important reality, for them and for their contemporary equivalents in the world's sole remaining superpower, is that Christ has died *for them* and has been raised *for them*. Perhaps in this chapter Paul is asking *us* to find our identity in relationship to the God who acted for us in Christ Jesus and not in our citizenship. I do not know whether that was a hard sell in Rome. I believe that it will be a hard sell now. But let us be very clear about this. Paul was intensely proud both of his Jewish heritage and his Roman citizenship. There can be no question, however, that it was *not* from these things that he drew his primary identity. It is not that this text asks us to deny our

---

[16] Throughout his letters Paul addresses the issue of the identity of the church as a corporate entity (Thompson, *Preaching Like Paul*, 93-98).

national identity. This text does tell us what our primary identity is, however, and compared to it our citizenship is incidental.

Identity is defined for a group in several ways; it is defined, for one, when a community shares a constitutive narrative. A constitutive narrative is a story that gives later generations a sense of belonging to a particular group and to which they refer constantly for guidance. The Bible as a whole is certainly the constitutive narrative for the Christian Church. Most particularly, Paul reminds his listeners here of the central part of the Christian story. It is so central that it is even summarized in the Apostles' Creed, "suffered under Pontius Pilate, crucified, dead and buried....the third day he rose again." Romans 5 invites us to imitate Paul in our preaching, to remind people of what they as Christians must surely have already heard, that Christ died *for us* in our helplessness and sin and that he has been raised in power to show us our salvation. Preaching, which recounts this story, or parts of it, and links it to contemporary reality gives identity to the church. We are what our stories tell us we are. Romans 5:1-11 reminds us to tell that story.

The idea of retelling the story to create identity is fashionable in contemporary homiletics. What is less fashionable is a second notion that Christian doctrine creates identity. That doctrine can have this capacity should hardly surprise us since many of our denominations are formally defined with respect to a particular statement of Christian doctrine. One thinks, for example, of Lutherans and the Augsburg Confession or Presbyterians and the Westminster Confession of Faith. Statements of faith are often now queried, rewritten, radically reinterpreted or, in practice, simply abandoned.

The mere fact that bodies of doctrine are now questioned should not, however, obscure the reality that for many centuries our denominations have found their identity in them. Paul is not a systematic theologian in the modern sense of the word. (It would be a gross anachronism to apply to him that fuzzy and trendy phrase "post-modern.") It may be, however, that theologians may be more sympathetic in our time to Paul than were our immediate forerunners. We might find a theology that grows in the interactions with very particular issues more sympathetic than a fully systematic theology. Christian belief that intersects with Christian life is for Paul the true mark of Christian identity. We also are what we believe.

This text asks us not only to tell that story but also to explain the theological significance of that story.[17] Or to put it more simply, it asks us to preach the doctrine of the atonement. It is not simply that Christ died—most people have. It is not even that Christ died unjustly and in a tragic and cruel manner. Millions have done the same. Paul here reminds the reader that the death of Christ was "for us," two of the most important words in the chapter.[18] Moreover, he died "for us" in our helplessness and in our alienation from God through sin. We were "enemies!" If it is a hard sell that we were "helpless," how much more will it be a hard sell that we were ever "enemies" of God. Surely the text invites us to

[17] "Stories may shape communal identity, but ultimately the cohesiveness of the community requires the interpretation of the communal story." Thompson, *Preaching Like Paul*, 12.

[18] See Karl Barth's magnificent rhapsody on these two words: "*For us*—that is, in so far as by His death we recognize the law of our own dying; in so far as in His death the invisible God becomes *for us* visible: in so far as His death is the place where atonement with God takes place." Karl Barth, *The Epistle to the Romans*, trans, Edwyn Hoslkyns (London, New York: Oxford University Press, 1933), 160.

adjust our concept of God away from an always kindly grandfather to something much more vivid and even dangerous. That is "God talk," the meaning of the word theology, in its purest form. This text invites us to reflect with our hearers on the significance of the death of Christ and what such a death says to us, both about God and ourselves. A preacher who takes the epistle to the Romans seriously must not be afraid of careful and disciplined theological reflection.

There is also a third mode of identity, the identity shaped by a set of practices. Once again, we can recognize this in our own collective pasts and to a lesser degree in our present. A generation ago, Roman Catholics did not eat fish on Friday. Even today, most Churches of Christ don't use instrumental music in worship. Strict fundamentalists of various churches do not dance or go to movies. Strict "justice Christians" of various groups might be people who buy their coffee from farmers' cooperatives in Central America. Paul might say something different: "Christians are the kind of people who present their bodies as a living sacrifice." But the principle remains intact. *We are what we do.* But as we have seen, this text is not *challenge,* but *confirmation.* Paul will not fully deal with our response to the good news declared in chapter 5 until chapter 12, so we will leave it aside for now.[19]

There is a problem here. Much preaching leaps over identities one and two and embraces identity number three. We are too eager to preach the identity that comes from certain practices and far too reluctant to preach the

---

[19] Paul does, however, deal in a preliminary way with questions of behavior appropriate to those who are in Christ in Romans 6.

grace that is the basis of Christian obligation. It is no accident that in common speech the words "sermon" and "preaching" have highly negative and heavily moralistic connotations. Nor is it simply a matter of common usage. One dictionary gives as the second meaning of homily, "tedious moralizing discourse."[20] A close reading of the letter to the Romans as a whole might be chiefly valuable to the contemporary preacher for what it teaches about the order of proclamation. Gospel comes first and obligation later. That ought to teach us something about what should hold priority in our preaching.

Preaching does well when it addresses identity. It may even do more; it may *create* identity. Churches are shaped by what they hear preached Sunday after Sunday. It could almost be said that Christian churches are what they hear preached. If they hear "tedious moralizing discourses" week after week, they become, almost inevitably, tedious moralists. But if they hear grace, there is at least the possibility that they will become grace-full. Paul seems to think that reminding the Romans of their true identity is vital. It's almost as if he thinks that if the Christian Church hears what it really is, it will become what it already is in Christ.

Perhaps Paul is on to something here. Perhaps preaching is not primarily a matter of telling people *what to do* but of reminding them *who they are*. We may be tempted to tell our people what they ought to be doing and, by heaven, what they ought *not* to be doing. Giving in to this temptation is, however, a mistake. We ought not address ethical questions, church problems, and social or

---

[20] *Concise Oxford English Dictionary.*

personal issues directly without first laying the theological groundwork for our preaching. Preaching Romans 5 is a vital part of that groundwork.

We then ask: *Is There a Movement Through the Text?*

There is clearly a movement implied by the text: from alienation and enmity to peace and reconciliation, from what we *were* to what we *are in Christ.* It may be that such a movement can provide a basic structure to a sermon. It should be noted that several key homileticians, most notably Eugene Lowry and Paul Wilson, suggest that a similar movement can serve as a standard pattern for effective Christian preaching. The movement may be labeled as law to gospel, judgment to grace,[21] or "oops" to "yeah,"[22] but the kinship to our text is clear. I do not believe that all sermons must follow this pattern, but where the text itself displays this kind of movement the sermon itself might well do so also.

*What Is God Doing In The Text?*

*Is God Doing Anything Similar In Our World?*

What God is doing in the text is crystal clear. God is justifying. God is proving his love for us in that while we were yet sinners, Christ died for us. Note that for the Romans all this is in the past. For them it happened long ago (at least a full generation) and far, far away. The question remains: "How are we 'saved' (v. 10) by a death and resurrection that happened very much long ago and

---

[21] Paul Wilson uses the law/gospel language in his older work, *Imagination of the Heart: New Understandings in Preaching* (Nashville: Abingdon, 1988). In his more recent work, *The Four Pages of the Sermon* (Nashville: Abingdon, 1999), Wilson has tended to use other language such as judgement/grace while retaining the basic movement.

[22] Eugene Lowry, *The Homiletical Plot: The Sermon as Narrative Art Form* (Atlanta: John Knox 1980). The book has very recently been reissued under the same title by Westminster John Knox.

far away?"[23] Is God doing the same thing in our world "for us?" Surely if we are Christians, the answer must be a resounding "Yes!" The text does indeed demand that we preach the atonement.

The issue might be raised in connection with an experience common to church people and to a number of non-church folk. Most of us are asked at one time or another, "Are you saved?" There is a biblically correct and theologically nuanced answer to that question: "I have been saved; I am being saved; and I will be saved." In order to save time, however, sometimes it is easier simply to answer, "Yes." The desire to save time may, however, be frustrated by a follow-up question: "When were you saved?" What the questioner really wants to know, of course, is: "When did you commit your life to the Lord Jesus Christ?" There are some problems with the question. Some of us can point to a specific time and place in answer. Others, raised in the faith since childhood may, despite a real and profound commitment, be unable to point to a particular moment in which they had become a Christian. More seriously, the primary focus in "being saved" ought not to fall only on our decision but on the work of Christ. There is a story that Karl Barth, too, was once asked when he was saved. He reportedly answered, "On a Friday afternoon, on a hill outside Jerusalem in about the year 30." Perhaps such an answer is not surprising from one whose first great work was a commentary on Romans. In any case, this particular text in Romans demands that we focus not on our decision but on Christ's work on the cross.

---

[23] A difficulty for preachers who are bound inescapably to the lectionary, the whole lectionary, and nothing but the lectionary is that it leaves out the second half of this chapter. It is in those verses that Paul attempts to answer the "how" question.

There are various explanations of the atonement that are reviewed in any introductory textbook. Christ's death on the cross is variously understood as the ransom of a prisoner, the manumission of a slave, the paying of a penalty in place of the guilty, the sacrifice of the paschal lamb, or a hero's victory over the power of evil. In the end, they are not really explanations but metaphors. The difficulty is that metaphors are like jokes. We either get them or we don't. But we keep on telling jokes, even though not everyone gets them and likewise we preachers keep on offering the metaphors in the hopes that our listeners will "get" or more properly "be got by" our metaphors. Some of the metaphors are culture-specific. Anselm's understanding that by his death Christ satisfied the offended honor of God is an example. Similarly, explanations of the death of Christ as an expression of solidarity with the lot of humans seem particularly bound to our own age. It may be more important to note here that in a period marked by narrative preaching we tend to expand metaphors into stories. We explain the meaning of Christ's death, insofar as an explanation is at all possible, by telling stories that may make the concept of a saving death credible to our listeners.

Here is a story I myself have used in a sermon. During the Second World War it was not just Jews who were sent to the Nazi concentration camps. In those dreadful camps were gypsies, homosexuals, Poles, communists, socialists, Protestants, Catholics, and people who had simply been in the wrong place at the wrong time. One such person was a Polish, Roman Catholic priest named Maximilian Kolbe. The Nazi guards became displeased with the prisoners in Maximilian Kolbe's hut for some reason and announced that they would immediately execute one out of ten prisoners, their names to be drawn by lot. One unlucky prisoner to whom the lot fell was a young Polish man, a husband, the father of young children. Maximilian Kolbe volunteered to take the young man's place and was executed.

Some years ago the Pope went back to Poland to declare Maximilian Kolbe a saint of the Roman Catholic Church. There was a special guest at the magnificent ceremony in his honor—an old Polish man, now a grandfather.

Of course he was there!

After all, wouldn't you be there? Wouldn't you be there at a ceremony in honor of somebody who died for you?

You are. Only, at this ceremony, you're the saint. Because, in truth, to be a saint you don't have to die for somebody. Somebody has to die for you. And he has.

This story and the many similar anecdotes used in our sermons attempt to seize the imagination rather than to appeal to the intellect of the listeners. No doctrine of the atonement is expressed, although a straightforward substitutionary theory might be implicit in it.

You might notice, however, that there is a serious theological and methodological problem here. The problem may be described in this way. For Paul, the story of the crucifixion and resurrection of Jesus Christ was clear. That story could be and indeed was used to elucidate the uncertainty and incomprehensibility of our present life. For contemporary preachers, however, the crucifixion and resurrection is unclear and in danger of appearing incomprehensible to our listeners. We therefore use stories from our present life to elucidate the significance of the cross and resurrection. There is a serious danger here. In our fervent desire to illuminate the cross, we may diminish the power of the cross to illuminate our lives. We may begin to treat the cross as a perplexing theological problem to be elucidated rather than as "ample proof to strengthen our minds with confidence in our salvation."[24]

I do not, nevertheless, suggest that we should cease telling stories. The story of Maximilian Kolbe may be understood not as an explanation of the cross of Christ but as a conscious imitation of it. It may therefore rightly find its place in Christian preaching. It cannot and must not take the place of preaching that centers, as does our text, on the death and resurrection of Jesus Christ. We may never so concentrate on Maximilian Kolbe or his like that we forget to say again and again, "at the right time Christ died for the ungodly."

This may be hard for us. We live in a society that values innovation and has a horror of "the same old thing." As a result, we preachers often feel pressured to "say something new" or at least to say the old thing in a new way. (A homiletician ought not to complain about this phenomenon. It helps keep us in business.) There can, however, be a real tyranny in this constant demand for innovation. In the early church, by contrast, innovation was not considered a positive value but rather a sign of unfaithfulness. Perhaps in our time we need to reclaim the sense of the early church—that the first duty of the preacher is faithfulness. Perhaps we also need a renewed confidence in the power of *the story*, not just any story, but *the story*, to grasp both those who know it well

---

[24] John Calvin, *The Epistles of Paul to the Romans and to the Thessalonians*, trans. Ross Mackenzie (Edinburgh: Oliver Boyd, 1960), 110.

and those who have never heard it before. We may also need a renewed confidence in our listeners' interest in and ability to comprehend our halting efforts to reflect on the significance of the story.

Such preaching might actually work. A recent graduate of the college where I teach became a minister of the Presbyterian church in a small Ontario town of about 2,000 people. He was blessed in his ministry by the presence in his little church of a man who had a passionate interest in children and youth and a gift for reaching out to them. Together they began a youth program that turned out to be amazingly successful. Soon they were drawing seventy-five or eighty kids to their program, attracting kids from beyond their own congregation and indeed from beyond any congregation in their small town. Some of these kids knew startlingly little about the Christian faith. One of these kids, Marty, when he first came into the church, looked at the ornate chairs at the front and asked, "Which chair does God sit in?" Marty might be a forerunner of many in our society for whom the story we tell will not be familiar.

Pete, the leader of the group, was a gifted storyteller. Sometimes they would build a campfire and Pete would dress up as a shepherd and tell Bible stories. One night Marty was present when Pete was telling the story of the death and resurrection of Christ. As Pete told the old, old story, the kids followed Jesus to Jerusalem. They watched him heal the sick and give sight to the blind. They listened as the rulers plotted to destroy and heard the tinkle of thirty pieces of silver. They sat with Jesus at a table in an upper room and followed him to the garden where he was betrayed with a kiss. They witnessed the trial, saw Peter deny Jesus, and heard the lash of the

Roman scourge. They stood by the foot of the cross and, in deepest silence, watched him die. Marty was transfixed. When Jesus, betrayed and abandoned, drew his last shuddering breath, Marty could take it no more. "Oh man-n-n!" he cried out in sorrow.

A child from the church, someone who already knew the story, was sitting next to Marty. He gently placed his hand on Marty's arm and said, "That's all right, Marty. The story isn't over yet."

We preachers have the inestimable privilege of telling that story and explaining its meaning. If we take up that privilege, our listeners, perhaps even the children, will be able to say to people in pain, "The story isn't over yet."

"But God proves his love for us in that while we still were sinners Christ died for us. Much more surely then, now that we have been justified by his blood, will we be saved through him from the wrath of God. For if while we were enemies, we were reconciled to God through the death of his Son, much more surely, having been reconciled, will we be saved by his life."

5

# Funding the Sermon with Gospeled Imagination:
Reflections on Text and Sermon from Romans
Mark Love

## The Mystery of the Sermon

I am convinced that the sermon is one of the great mysteries of the universe. It submits to no laws. Were it only true that a good sermon could be produced with concentrated effort! Every preacher knows the humbling experience of confidently striding into the pulpit with a fool-proof sermon tucked neatly in the pages of a well-worn Bible only to have it die somewhere in the second move. Every preacher has also experienced the agony and ecstasy of sermon preparation. Some sermons appear willingly on the page, yielding easily to the pen as it moves across paper. A bare reading of the text touches some latent but fully formed inspiration in the mind of the preacher so that the sermon flows from some effortless homiletical font—more glorious even still when the invitation song comes immediately to mind! These sermons seem to pre-exist somewhere in the collected imagination of the preacher. In moments like these, nothing can stand in the way of the sermon—not exegetical insight, nor twenty-plus centuries of Christian thought, nor even a direct revelation from God.

Other weeks the sermon is nowhere to be found. *Nothing* comes to mind. Inspiration is on the lam. The text in view may be choice, rich with themes for exposition, and still no sermon is to be found. These are the weeks we scrub our method a little harder. Off the shelf comes Arndt-Gingrich, TDNT, critical commentary, or if the preacher has no shame, Lucado or Swindoll! These are the weeks we strain over our focus and function statements, hoping that clarity and focus will stand in for engaging and moving. We pray for ice storms.

These opening words form a cautionary introduction to the assignment of this essay. I was asked to write something about the move from text to sermon, particularly in light of what Paul does in the letter to the Romans. The very phrase "move from text to sermon" betrays a confidence in method or process in producing a good sermon. When I began my ministry training, I was taught to trust in the discipline of my methodology. Given the appropriate exegetical method, one could confidently extract the meaning of a given text. The move to the sermon was relatively simple, in theory. The preacher simply walked the message, or abiding principle, across the bridge between the ancient and contemporary worlds, dressed it with illustrations, and ended with a poem. Well, we've come some ways since then. We have moved well beyond the modern conceit of the detached observer. We recognize that the preacher is more than just a scientist who, through the use of an exact method, extracts a pure message. Not only does the preacher bring values, experiences, and impressions, which cannot *and should not* be expunged, but the very method trusted to provide a value-less posture is itself laden with values and assumptions.

Recent homiletical studies have tried to expand our notions of what it means to engage a text. Thomas Long has taught us a great deal about the function of a text. The text not only has a message but a form that causes it to act a certain way and thereby produce a particular experience in the reader/hearer.[1] Stephen Farris has also helped us think about the move from text to sermon by focusing on analogies. He provides preachers with a series of questions with which to quiz our exegetical findings in order to provide points of contact with modern listeners.[2] I teach my students to think about the oppositions that might keep the text from being heard or experienced. What obstacles kept the first listeners from hearing the text? What obstacles, such as obscurity, familiarity, and scandal, stand in our way? All of these ways of thinking are designed to construct a bridge so that the text can speak to the contemporary listener. Moreover, these suggestions are helpful and keep the text in a place of primacy in the homiletical conversation.

However, I find the image of a bridge problematic in adequately describing the relationship between text and sermon and, indeed, may have instincts that run counter to what we find in the text itself.[3] As suggested

---

[1] Thomas G. Long, *The Witness of Preaching* (Louisville, Ky: Westminster/John Knox Press, 1994), and *Preaching and the Literary Forms of the Bible* (Philadelphia: Fortress Press, 1989).

[2] Stephen Farris, *Preaching that Matters: The Bible and Our Lives* (Louisville, Ky: Westminster/John Knox Press, 1998), 75-124.

[3] In conversation on this point, Farris agrees that the bridge image is limited and is reluctant to use this language to describe the relationship between

somewhat fancifully in the opening lines of this essay, I don't think the bridge notion fully accounts for the actual mystery of putting a sermon together. I think, in some ways, the bridge theory of sermon construction participates in the same modernist conceit we see with regard to exegetical method. The bridge can be thought of as this exacting methodology—something we construct beginning from the side of the text so that ideally the traffic is all one-way. Again, we talk about moving from text to sermon—one-way traffic—forgetting that there is also a preacher. It is stating the obvious to suggest that given the same text, the same exegetical method, and the same hermeneutical process by which a bridge is constructed, two preachers will still come up with two radically different sermons—different not only in focus and function, but in theology as well. The $x$ factor is the preacher himself and a methodology sometimes is not nearly powerful enough to override what a preacher brings to the sermon. This is not a startling or new insight. Long, Farris, and others have recognized this phenomenon. If there is a bridge, the preacher stands simultaneously on both sides—with the text and with a contemporary audience. And if there is traffic on the bridge, it moves both ways simultaneously.[4]

---

text and sermon. (Unfortunately, his editor chose to put the picture of a bridge on the front cover of *Preaching that Matters*). Still, Farris' book describes a process that is very "bridge-like." Though nuanced, Farris' proposal still displays the classic move from what the text meant to what the text means. However, it should also be pointed out that it was Farris' suggestions in a recent essay that got me thinking outside of the "bridge box." See "Limping Away With a Blessing: Biblical Studies and Preaching at the End of the Second Millennium," *Interpretation* (October, 1987):358-70.

[4] As will be commented on later, the "bridge theory" of sermon construction has come under recent critique, most notably by David Buttrick, *A Captive Voice: The Liberation of Preaching* (Louisville, Ky: Westminster/John

The "bridge theory" of sermon construction recommends itself at the level of keeping the text in an authoritative position. By insisting that the sermon proceed from the text to the contemporary listener, the primacy of the text is upheld. Ironically, this way of thinking about sermons may not be very biblical. The bridge theory does not correspond to the instincts of biblical writers and preachers in their appropriation of biblical texts. Could Paul, from the book of Romans, sharpen our understandings of the relationship between the text and sermon in a way that makes better sense of the mystery of sermon preparation?

## *Paul as Preacher*

Joseph Fitzmyer says in the introduction to his commentary on Romans, "Paul's style is more that of an orator than of a writer. It is clear that he has dictated the text of Romans, and in this he is the preacher."[5] James Thompson also sees Paul in his letters as more than a writer. Thompson suggests that we can learn a great deal about early Christian preaching by noticing how Paul argues in his letters.

> Although Paul and others in antiquity distinguished between the written and spoken word and preferred the latter, we can nevertheless conclude that Paul's letters provided the

Knox Press, 1994), and Edward Farley, "Toward a New Paradigm for Preaching," *Preaching as a Theological Task: Word, Gospel, Scripture*, In Honor of David Buttrick, Thomas G. Long and Edward Farley, eds. (Louisville, Ky: Westminster/John Knox Press, 1996), 165-75.

[5] Joseph A. Fitzmyer, *Romans*, The Anchor Bible (New York: Doubleday, 1994), 92.

occasion for *hearing*. This collection of letters, written as a substitute for his presence and read orally in the assembly, provides an insight into the scope of his preaching ministry. If the letters contain what he would have said if he had been present, they offer insights into the principles of arrangement, modes of argumentation, and stylistic features of the Pauline sermon.[6]

While this thesis has the disadvantage of not having any of Paul's actual sermons with which to compare letters like Romans, Thompson is convincing at several points. Paul, in his letters, ought to be taken seriously as a model for preaching. While Thompson focuses on Paul's preaching role as rhetor, evangelist, and pastor, I would like to suggest that we can learn something about preaching and the mystery of sermon construction by observing how Paul relates to texts. To do this, we must bring into view some of the text of Romans.

## Paul's Pastoral Strategy

Romans is a pastoral document.[7] In other words, Romans was written to deal with church trouble, perhaps to bring unity to a church divided along Jew/Gentile lines.[8] The point to make here, within the limits of this

---

[6] James W. Thompson, *Preaching Like Paul: Homiletical Wisdom for Today* (Louisville, Ky: Westminster/John Knox Press, 2001), 35-36.

[7] See James W. Thompson, "Reading Romans Today," *Leaven* (Winter, 2000) 8:197-200. Thompson suggests that recent scholarship on Romans tends to see the letter's purpose primarily in pastoral terms.

[8] See James Walters' excellent discussion in *Ethnic Issues in Paul's Letter to the Romans: Changing Self-Definitions in Earliest Roman Christianity* (Valley Forge, PA.: Trinity Press International, 1993).

essay, is that Romans is not abstract doctrine, or even credentialing doctrine; it is practical theology constructed for a particular context. Romans is theology for the purpose of addressing a particular problem in a congregation of God's people.

So, Paul's letter needs to accomplish something—and with a church he did not establish and has never visited. His standing and credibility must be established early and with broad appeal. His opening words must convey trustworthy and authoritative intentions. He must put across, in his own self-introduction, both authority and promise. He needs to signal on what basis he speaks and what he intends to say.

The opening verses of Romans, therefore, are very important. Paul presents himself as a gospeled person and as a gospeler. Notice how prominent the word "gospel" is in these verses.

> Paul, a slave of Jesus Christ, called to be an apostle, set apart for the *gospel* of God...
>
> The *gospel* concerning his Son who was descended from David according to the flesh and was declared to be Son of God with power according to the Spirit...
>
> For God, whom I serve with my spirit by announcing the *gospel* of his Son...
>
> Hence my eagerness to proclaim the *gospel* to you also who are in Rome...
>
> I am not ashamed of the *gospel*; it is the power of God for salvation for everyone who has faith...(1:1,3-4,9,15,16).

The introduction to Romans provides a glimpse of the direction Paul intends to go in addressing congregational concerns. The strong statement of belief in 1:16-17 serves as a hinge to connect the body of the letter to the introduction. Paul is signaling his desire to address the congregational issues facing the church in Rome with the resources of the gospel, for it is the power of God for salvation, for the Jew first and the Greek also.

Paul's understanding of the gospel reaches its pastoral conclusion in 15:7, "Welcome one another, therefore, just as Christ has welcomed you for the glory of God." The mutual welcome to be extended between Jew and Gentile finds its ethical charter in Paul's understandings of gospel. A gospel of grace and faith leaves no room for boasting. All have sinned and are under the dominion of death, Jew and Gentile alike. All are enemies for whom Christ died. Indeed, for Paul the death and resurrection of Jesus marks the beginning of a new age with new possibilities for humankind. As people live out the implications of their baptisms, as they learn what it means to be dead to sin and alive to God by the power of the Spirit, they will become a new creation. And this will not only create better individuals, but lead to a new kind of community—one that does not boast of human merit, ethnicity, or priority of relationship, but one that practices the welcome of God in Jesus toward one another. To the extent that the death and resurrection of Jesus creates these realities among the Christians in Rome, the righteousness of God will be revealed.

Paul writes Romans as a gospeler. The church in Rome needs help, and Paul offers what he has been given—the death and resurrection of Jesus. If Paul is a pastoral theologian, it is as a result of his understanding of the cross. He reads the congregational situation in Rome through the lenses of the Christ event. I would like to suggest that as a preacher he reads Scripture the same way.

## *Paul, Text, and Sermon*

To the extent, and it is to a great extent, that Paul uses traditional materials, (i.e., Scripture), we see him negotiate text and sermon. We watch him do hermeneutics. We witness his work in applying Scripture, namely the Old Testament, to the new circumstances of the Gentile mission. Canon critics, like Brevard Childs and especially James Sanders, have opened our eyes to the fact that the biblical authors do hermeneutics. They creatively appropriate texts from a different era to bring a living word to God's people in light of new circumstances. Sanders suggests that we can learn what it means to speak to our own situations by learning how the biblical authors used texts to speak to theirs.[9] No one gives us a better opportunity to do this than Paul.

While Paul's use of the Old Testament is complex and the topic upon which a great deal of scholarship has focused, I think a few obvious observations are in order. First, Paul made use of several different reading strategies. He practiced more than one way of reading Scripture. Moreover, his reading strategy was not determined by the form of the text. For example, in both Romans and Galatians he makes use of the Abraham/Sarah stories. In Romans, he takes a fairly literal tack. In Galatians, he reads the story allegorically. Sometimes Paul seems

---

[9] James Sanders, *Canon and Community: A Guide to Canonical Criticism* (Eugene, OR: Wipf and Stock Publishers, 1984), and *Torah and Canon* (Eugene, OR: Wipf and Stock Publishers, 1984).

interested in the original context, sometimes not. Sometimes Paul uses a Psalm as an invitation to praise. Sometimes he uses a Psalm to make a fairly rational argument. He is not bound to form.[10]

Second, Paul's goal in his letters is not to take a text and illumine it. He does not model for us good preaching. Certainly, we are limited here by not knowing Paul's preaching strategies over time. His extended stays in Corinth or Ephesus may very well have been spent in some verse-by-verse exposition of Scripture.[11] But if his letters, as Thompson suggests, can be read as sermons, then this is not always a concern of his. Scripture, while highly authoritative for Paul, often serves as subtext rather than text. Paul seems interested in exposing something greater than the text.

Finally, Paul's use of Scripture does not yield to the bridge theory of sermon construction. It seems that what the text meant or how it functioned is of secondary importance to what the text means in light of his new reading of the work of God in and through Christ Jesus. He does not move from text to contemporary setting. In fact, if there is a bridge, Paul might very well be working backward from contemporary setting to ancient text.

Some might be quick to point out here that Paul is not a model for us with regard to use of Scripture since he was an inspired apostle and we are not. Therefore,

---

[10] David Bartlett takes notice of several different reading strategies employed by New Testament authors and suggests that to be biblical may very well include an openness to a variety of ways to read the text. *Between the Bible and the Church: New Methods for Biblical Preaching* (Nashville: Abingdon, 1999), 11-35.

[11] Richard Hays states succinctly that Paul's characteristic style of exposition was not "line by line decoding." *Echoes of Scripture in the Letters of Paul,* (New Haven, CT: Yale University Press, 1989), 155.

different rules apply to us. I would certainly recognize a difference—but it is a difference of degree and not kind. Paul is like the answers found in the back of the book to the math questions we worked in high school. We check our work against his to see if we are doing it correctly. However, there are some problems unique to our context for which there will not be specific Pauline answers in the back of the book. To be faithful to Paul will mean precisely that we have learned to do theology like he does. In fact, this is precisely what I'm arguing. Paul does not model for us a particular method, but rather a theological stance that enables a preacher to move confidently between text and sermon.

Some become nervous when we let loose of method as a boundary. What will keep us from abusing Scripture, having it say whatever we want it to? Won't we just slide into relativism? Let me be clear here. I am not calling for an abandoning of disciplined exegesis or an ignoring of issues of form and function. I am not proposing doing away with expository preaching. I simply want us to see that method does not function for Paul, or for us, as the guarantor of faithful sermons. Paul is not, at least not primarily, a preacher of texts. Paul is a preacher of the gospel. We see from texts like Romans 1 that Paul reads both ministry and Scripture through the lenses of the death and resurrection of Jesus. His "bridge" between text and context is not methodological but theological. This approach is not relativistic. Paul's use of Scripture in preaching is bounded by his understanding of what God has accomplished in the death and resurrection of Jesus.

## Scripture, the Sermon, and Theological Imagination

At its most basic level, the gospel is the announcement that God has acted decisively in the death and resurrection of Jesus. The gospel cannot be reduced to a single telling nor to a single interpretation of that event. The messages and meanings that proceed from the event are numerous. The question is, "How does the event become a message?"

For Paul, the announcement becomes a message in relation to two things: context and Scripture. Context forces Paul to think creatively. He is constantly thinking, "How does the death and resurrection apply to this situation?" This is imaginative work, not in the sense that it is made up, but in the sense that various elements are woven together in creative and dynamic ways.

But Paul is not simply moving here from event to context. He has a primary dialogue partner. Jesus died in accordance with the Scriptures—and it's well worth exploring what this means for Paul. His preaching imagination is funded by the story of Israel. He does not look for precedents or primary resonances in any other story. His narrative world, from which he preaches, is mapped with the images of Abraham, Moses, Jeremiah, and the like.[12]

Richard Hays has written persuasively concerning the "whispered or unstated correspondences between Paul's text and Scripture." These correspondences "generate

---

[12] See Ben Witherington, III, *Paul's Narrative Thought World: The Tapestry of Tragedy and Triumph* (Louisville: Westminster/John Knox Press, 1994).

new meanings and suggest more than they assert." They grow out of the "subconscious structural parallels between Paul's message (word of the cross) and Scripture." Paul "seems to have leaped—in moments of metaphorical insight—to intuitive apprehensions of the meanings of texts without the aid or encumbrance of systematic reflection about his own hermeneutics."[13] Hays' statement confirms my opening assertion about sermons—that some of them leap at the preacher from someplace other than a methodology. They come from an intuitive place, a place preformed within the preacher's theological imagination. These intuitions should certainly be quizzed and disciplined, but they should also be honored and allowed.

While Paul's primary conversation partner in contextualizing the gospel is Scripture, his reading of Scripture is by necessity imaginative and his reading strategies numerous. This imaginative reading stance in relation to the text owes much to Paul's apocalyptic framework for understanding the work of God. The death and resurrection of Jesus has marked a decisive turn of the ages. As Hays suggests, "(Paul) believes himself, along with his churches, to stand in a privileged moment in which the clutter of past texts and experiences assumes a configuration of eschatological significance."[14] This privileged moment marks a new age, not simply an extension or logical outcome of the previous age. It is an invasion of the old age, an intrusion on the way things have been. Paul does not see the new age as a recapitulation of creation. He envisions the work of God emerging

---

[13] Hays, *Echoes of Scripture*, 161.

[14] Hays, *Echoes of Scripture*, 165.

under the influence of the Christ event as nothing less than a new creation. As Leander Keck summarizes Paul's thinking, "The age to come is not the outgrowth of the past and present, not the consummation or telos of history, but the God-given alternative to it."[15]

Paul simply does not read Scripture in a straight line. He reads it backward from the cross. The word of the cross becomes a sponge, which absorbs images, stories, and fragments from Scripture and recasts them in light of the new work of God. Again, this is imaginative work, and I think Paul would say it allows for a variety of reading perspectives and strategies.[16] Again, Paul's faithfulness in relation to the text is not bounded by his methodology, but by his theological vision of the death and resurrection of Jesus.

So, the question of the relationship between the text and sermon must be asked well in advance of the Monday morning reading of next Sunday's text.[17] The prior formation of the minister's theological imagination is critical. The relationship between text and sermon is mediated by the preacher's theological imagination. The vital question for preaching then is, "What funds the minister's theological imagination?"

---

[15] Leander Keck, "Paul as Thinker," *Interpretation* (January, 1993: 47:1):31.

[16] See James L. Kay, "The Word of the Cross at the Turn of the Ages," *Interpretation* (January, 1999) 53: 44-56. Kay describes the work of the preacher in an apocalyptic framework as an exercise in stereoscopic imagination.

[17] Buttrick, Long, and Farley have been critical of lectionary approaches to preaching that begin with the selection of a text. See footnote 19 for complete citation.

## *The Funded Imagination*

Too often ministers fund their imaginations for preaching from wells that are dry holes, theologically speaking. Frankly, the bridge theory of producing sermons has unwittingly encouraged preachers to cast about for something that will hold a congregation's attention for the duration of a sermon. The type of work done by exegetes represented in critical commentaries leaves the average preacher a long way from an actual sermon. Discouraged at the prospect of having to represent what the text meant in its original context, a simultaneously ponderous and inexact science, preachers turn to pop psychology or principles for success with the lesser challenge of providing a proof text. As a result, preachers often read more in the story of the predominant culture than they do in the story of the faith. The preaching imagination must be formed by a thorough immersion in the sources of the Christian story.

Though no one would plead guilty to complicity in this crime, the bridge theory of sermon construction may also have contributed to an understanding of sermon preparation in which God is unnecessary. André Resner suggests that "overconfident opinions about what our fastidious uses of methodology can accomplish threaten the whole process of studying the Bible for preaching."[18] Many observers have recently argued that "a rigid historical-critical descriptive approach overlooks the canon's function as revelation in the

---

[18] Andre Resner, "At Cross Purposes: Gospel, Scripture, and Experience in Preaching," *Preaching Autobiography: Connecting the World of the Preacher and the World of the Text*, Rochester College Lectures on Preaching, vol 2 (Abilene, TX: ACU Press, 2001), 59.

community of faith."[19] Simply put, it is God who is to be searched for in Scripture, not an original meaning or abstract principle concerning God. And it is primarily participation in the life of God that makes meanings possible, not reading methodologies.[20]

Too often, the bridge theory encourages readers to think of the Bible as an object to be mastered rather than as a living word through which God speaks directly to his church. It is clear from Paul's uses of the text that he reads Scripture as direct address to his contemporary situation. This can be seen, for instance, in his fascinating use of the Exodus tradition in 1 Corinthians 10. After reciting elements of the story, Paul writes, "These things happened to them to serve as an example, and they were written down for us, on whom the end of the ages has come" (10:11). Paul's eschatological frame allows him to read Scripture with immediacy. Scripture is not primarily a word to a historical "them" which we overhear, but a word to "us" who live in the fullness of God's work in Jesus Christ. For Paul "the word is near you, in your mouth, and in your heart" (Rom 10:8). For Paul, the word of God in Scripture is both durable and flexible, which allows it to speak in varying contexts with a creative immediacy.

---

[19] Paul Scott Wilson, "Biblical Studies and Preaching: A Growing Divide?" *Preaching as a Theological Task: Word, Gospel, Scripture,* In Honor of David Buttrick, Thomas G. Long and Edward Farley, eds. (Louisville, Ky: Westminster/John Knox Press, 1996), 144. Wilson cites R. E. Clements, Paul D. Hanson, Brevard S. Childs, and Walter Brueggemann as scholars who, in different ways, remind readers that it is important to read the Bible as Scripture.

[20] See here Farris' excellent conclusions in "Limping Away with a Blessing," *Interpretation* vol. 51 (1997), 367. "Any method of interpretation will suffice as long as it is God to whom we are listening in these texts" (367). While I would argue that some reading strategies are better than others, his emphasis on wrestling with God as more important than methodology is a point well-taken.

A more functional notion of reading the Bible as Scripture, as a word of nearness, would bring the God who stands in and behind the text into clearer view. This in turn requires the preacher to bring spiritual disciplines to the text, along with his lexicon and Bible dictionary, what Resner refers to as a "spirituality of reading."[21] Hays, reflecting upon Paul's relationship to Scripture, suggests that true interpretation does not depend on "historical inquiry nor on erudite literary analysis," but on being attentive to the promptings of the Spirit.[22] The prospect of meeting the living God in the reading of Scripture necessitates a certain openness to new possibilities. The preaching imagination begins with a commitment to reading the Bible as Scripture.

Earlier in this essay, I suggested that Paul is less interested in preaching texts than he is in the gospel. This might sound like permission to spend less time with the text. However, this shift from preaching texts to preaching gospel does not require *less* attention to the text, but a *different kind* of attention.[23] P. T. Forsyth saw

---

[21] Resner, "At Cross Purposes,"61.

[22] Hays, *Echoes of Scripture*, 156.

[23] Buttrick and Farley have both proposed that the selection of a text might actually inhibit the preaching of the gospel. As Farley suggests, not every text illumines the gospel, and too many expository sermons dwell in the text's history without allowing the gospel its say in a contemporary situation ("Toward a New Paradigm" 172). However, without the disciplined selection of a variety of texts for preaching, the "cosmos" of Scripture remains a formless void in the imagination of the congregation. It is precisely the "otherness" of Scripture that allows God to confront our cultural accommodations and give room for the gospel to be heard. What is needed is not a retreat from taking texts as the genesis of a sermon, but a theologically disciplined and imaginative reading of those texts in light of contemporary circumstances. See Ronald J. Allen, "Why Preach from Passages in the Bible?" *Preaching as a Theological Task: Word, Gospel, Scripture*, In Honor of David Buttrick, Thomas G. Long and Edward Farley, eds. (Louisville, Ky: Westminster/John Knox Press, 1996), 176-88.

long ago that the Bible needs to be rescued from atomistic readings, "which reduce it to a religious scrap book."

> The Bible is much more than a collection of spiritual apophthegms, or the gnomic *reliquiae* of moral sages. And a great part of the preacher's work is to rescue the Bible from this treatment, which is largely due to textual preaching, and is part of the price we pay for it. He must cultivate more the free, large, and organic treatment of the Bible, where each part is valuable for its contribution to a living, evangelical whole....[24]

As Forsyth points out, the Bible does not merely describe a distant world from a time long ago, it "has a world and a context of its own. It has an ethos, if not a cosmos of its own."[25] The preacher must dwell in the living pages of Scripture in order for a theological imagination to take root.

Annie Dillard describes this "dwelling" well.

> The Bible, this ubiquitous, persistent black chunk of a bestseller is a chink—often the only chink—through which winds howl. It is a singularity, a black hole into which our rich and multiple world strays and vanishes. We crack open its pages at our peril. Many educated, urbane, and flourishing experts in every aspect of business, culture, and science have felt pulled by

---

[24] P. T. Forsyth, *Positive Preaching and the Modern Mind* (Grand Rapids: Eerdmans, 1907), 19.

[25] Forsyth, *Positive Preaching*, 20.

this anachronistic, semibarbaric mass of antique laws and fabulous tales from far away; they entered its queer, strait gates and were lost. Eyes open, heads high, in full possession of their critical minds, they obeyed the high, inaudible whistle, and let the gates close behind them.

Every summer we memorized [Bible verses] at camp. Every Sunday at home in Pittsburgh, we heard these things in Sunday school. Every Thursday we studied these things, and memorized them, too (strictly as literature they said), at our private school. I had miles of Bible in memory: some perforce, but most by hap, like the words to songs. There was no corner of my brain where you could not find, among the files of clothing labels and heaps of rocks and minerals, among the swarms of protozoans and shelves of novels, whole tapes and snarls and reels of Bible. I wrote poems in deliberate imitation of its sounds, those repeated feminine endings followed by thumps, or those long hard beats followed by softness. Selah.[26]

The poems Dillard describes belong to a long sojourn with the text, a habitation, in which she has learned to speak in the primary cadences, idioms, and fragments of Scripture. She, like Paul, speaks in echoes and allusions. Preaching, whether it takes a text or not, should do the same thing. It should allow listeners to dwell imaginatively in a world not given to them by the principalities and powers of this age. If Forsyth is correct

---

[26] Annie Dillard, "The Book of Luke," *The Annie Dillard Reader* (New York: Harper/Collins, 1994), 266, 268.

in asserting that the Bible has its own cosmos, then for the minister to fund the preaching imagination anywhere else limits the world Scripture would reveal from being seen.

This dwelling with Scripture, however, must do more than seek to imitate "feminine endings and thumps." Scripture verses can be quoted to support nearly any theological program. The preacher must learn not only to speak like Scripture, but also to think like Scripture. Here the work of canon critics like Sanders becomes indispensable. When we take up Scripture we enter a conversation well under way. Scripture has certain instincts about how to apply and reapply traditions over time and how to think about wisdom traditions outside of Israel's story. Some words are more authoritative than others, and some theological perspectives can only be appropriated faithfully when held in tension with others. This type of reading of Scripture requires more than just text—scientists looking for historical fact and grammatical pattern. The reader who dwells in the text must be a theologian, not just an exegete.

Finally, a gospeled imagination springs from devoted attention to the meaning of the death and resurrection of Jesus. For many of us, the word of the cross has been limited to a narrow range of understandings of the atonement. But for Paul, the death and resurrection becomes the lens through which he views all of life. It informs his understandings of ministry, community, marriage, and human possibility. More importantly, through the cross he claims knowledge and experience of God and trusts the leading of the Spirit. As Forsyth observed of Paul, we must all fasten on the cross and press every ounce of divine life from it for our

healing.[27]   Our churches are malnourished for lack of
feeding on Christian wisdom, wisdom that finds both its
rudiment and profundity in the death and resurrection of
Jesus. Like Paul, every preacher should seek to elucidate
more than the meaning of a given text. Every text and
every sermon should serve the interests of the gospel.

## *Conclusion*

In the movie, "A Knight's Tale," knights joust to the
strains of contemporary rock and roll. Characters
in medieval garb function as odd contemporaries,
competing to the metal anthems "We Will Rock You,"
and "Taking Care of Business." The movie does
not depict an ancient setting, but neither is it simply
contemporary. The genre of movie has created an
imaginative setting in which a temporal warp allows the
viewer to stand in various worlds simultaneously. *Good
preaching does the same thing.* The genre of gospel, a
dramatic turning of the ages, allows the preacher to stand
in a new world, neither ancient nor of this age, but a
world of the gospel's own imagination. The sermon is an
intertextual web that brings into creative interplay the
echoes and allusions of Scripture, the contexts of
contemporary communities, and the instincts of the
death and resurrection of Jesus. Under the influence of
the gospel, the sermon insists on speaking, even if
somewhat anachronistically, in the present tense.

This kind of "preaching" can be seen in the
letters of Paul, Romans serving as a classic example. Paul's
use of texts is very different than what is described in

---

[27] Forsyth, *Positive Preaching*, 17.

typical bridge theories of sermon construction. The faithfulness of his proclamation is not bounded by method, or by particular reading strategies. Rather, his faithfulness in preaching is theologically bounded by his understandings of the Christ event. As Hays suggests,

> Paul's readings of Scripture enact a certain imaginative vision of the relation between Scripture and God's eschatological activity in the present time. To learn from Paul how to read Scripture is to learn to share that vision, so that we can continue to read and speak under the guidance of the Spirit, interpreting Scripture in light of the gospel and the gospel in light of Scripture.[28]

Therefore, Paul does serve as a preaching model, not just as a rhetor, pastor, or evangelist, but as one who uses texts in preaching. To the extent that the preacher's theological imagination is funded in the same manner as Paul's, the preacher is permitted to read Scripture in the same imaginative way he does. The move away from a bridge understanding of sermon construction may open the way for preaching to rediscover its apocalyptic birthright, and, in turn, to offer the preacher permission to exercise theological imagination.

---

[28] Hays, *Echoes of Scripture*, 183.

# II

Part 2:

*Sermons on Romans*

# 6

## Sermons from Romans 1-8
Mike Cope

### Romans 1:18-2:11
### Introductory Comments

James Walters has long informed my thinking on Romans. In Chapter One of this book, Walters argues succinctly that the primary concern in Romans is not justification by faith. The primary concern is the relationship between Christian Jews and Gentiles. Paul believes that both groups suffered from a superiority complex. Paul must demonstrate how neither group has any room for boasting. The following sermon highlights this major concern that Paul had in writing the letter to the Romans.

I've attempted to help listeners hear this text through the image of darkness. Paul says that "their foolish hearts were darkened." That sparked the sermonic movement for me: from the darkness of others (1:18-32) to the darkness within us (2:1-11) to the unifying light that comes only in the gospel of Christ.

## *"Midnight in the Garden of Evil"* *Romans 1:18-2:11*

*O God, our Creator and Redeemer, we ask you today for light to see the darkness all around us and within us. Please pour through me the gift of preaching so that we can see our common desperation and our common hope through Jesus Christ. Use these words to bind us together through your words of conviction and grace. In Christ our Redeemer we pray, Amen.*

What would you like to say to a church that is struggling for unity? How about, "be nice"? "play fair"? "be tolerant"?

To just such a church, Paul goes straight to the deep well of theology: "God does not show favoritism." That's the conclusion of this morning's text. But he has a funny way of getting to that conclusion!

Behind this morning's text, I'm confident there was another text in Paul's mind. When he penned these cage-rattling words about the plight of humans, these words may well have been stirring in his mind:

> In the beginning God created the heavens and the earth. Now the earth was formless and empty, darkness was over the surface of the deep, and the Spirit of God was hovering over the waters. And God said, "Let there be light," and there was light. God saw the light was good, and he separated the light from the darkness. (Gen 1ff.)

In that pristine moment when God created, there was light. But since that time, because of rebellion by those made in his image, great darkness had set over the land. A darkness of fear. A darkness of confusion. But mostly a darkness of wickedness.

### (Im)Moral Midnight

When Elie Wiesel wrote his horrible memories of life in a concentration camp, he could only call it *Night*. He saw all the Jews in his village prodded into cattle cars, stripped of their possessions and their dignity. He saw a mother, a little sister, and all his family herded into an oven. He saw babies pitchforked, children hanged, and adults cooked.

> Never shall I forget that night, seven times cursed and seven times sealed. Never shall I forget that smoke. Never shall I forget the little faces of the children, whose bodies I saw turned into wreaths of smoke beneath a silent blue sky. Never shall I forget that nocturnal silence which deprived me, for all eternity, of the desire to live. Never shall I forget those moments which murdered my God and my soul and turned my dreams to dust. Never shall I forget these things, even if I am condemned to live as long as God himself. Never.

This is midnight in the garden of evil. It's not dusk. It's not just late. It is midnight.

But what does this moral midnight look like? The evidence is all around us—perhaps even within us!—but Paul *shows* us. With his high-speed film and his tripod, he offers us this stunning picture of midnight.

There is depraved thinking and depraved behavior. There is every imaginable (and perhaps some unimaginable) wickedness: envy, murder, strife, deceit, malice, and so on. Not only do people *do* wicked things, they even offer their stamp of approval for others in their moral pigpens.

Paul especially underscores the sexual immorality all around. People degrade their bodies with one another. They stray far from the biblical ideal of chastity, which is abstinence in singleness and fidelity in marriage (the covenanted relationship between a man and woman). They even exchange natural desires for unnatural ones.

Now—doesn't this make you angry? Doesn't it make you mad at what's happening around us? Doesn't it make you upset with public officials who commit adultery and lie? Doesn't it infuriate you with homosexuals and a gay agenda? Wouldn't you love to give someone a piece of your mind?

### Whiplash

Then you got caught by Paul's trap. For just about the time he has us whipped into a frenzy, just when we're ready to form a moral posse to crusade for Christ, he jerks us so abruptly we get whiplash!

"You, therefore, have no excuse, you who pass judgment on someone else, for at whatever point you judge the other, you are condemning yourself, because you who pass judgment do the same things" (2:1). Ouch!

Do you remember the comeback on the playground when someone called you a bad name? The highly enlightened response was: "Takes one to know one!" I think here Paul uses the "takes-one-to-know-one" argument. It's not my brother, not my sister, but it's me, O Lord, standing in the need of prayer.

There's plenty of darkness within all of us. We can all confess to stubbornness and unrepentant hearts.

And, oddly enough, in this very confession, there is a basis for unity in a church. For we all have the same problem (darkness from sin and separation) and the same need (redemption).

### Why Is It Midnight?

But how did it get so dark? Where did this midnight come from? You have to read the text carefully. Otherwise, you might assume it got to be so dark *because* of all the wickedness. In other words, you might suppose that people were so wicked that God gave them up and poured out his wrath. But according to Paul, moral perversion is the *result* of God's wrath, not the reason for it.

Why is everything in chaos? Because God gave them up—as verses 24, 26, and 28 keep telling us. So why, then, did God give them up? This is where the Genesis story comes in. Some things about God are evident. But despite that enlightenment, people didn't glorify the Creator or thank him. The proper response to creation would have been worship and gratitude. But people chose instead to worship *what* was made rather than the *one* who made it all.

The central sin, then, was idolatry: trying to find life in someone or something other than God. It lies at the root of our alienation from God and from one another. Full of selfishness and pride, eager to be in the know, longing to be independent and to trust no one, we have rebelled. All these sins catalogued by Paul are merely the symptoms. The real virus is idolatry. Simply put, we forget that we (or other people or things) are not God.

So God allows the irony of sin to run full course: our desire for self-promotion ends in self-destruction. We demanded our own way, so he stepped back. C. S. Lewis was right on target when he wrote that people will "enjoy forever the horrible freedom they have demanded, and are therefore self-enslaved."

Homosexuality receives so much attention here from Paul, not because it's the worst sin, but because it's a better illustration of what's gone wrong. Using words that come from the Greek translation of Genesis 1 for "male" and "female," Paul spotlights homosexual behavior as a rejection of God's design for his creation. It is a clear indication that we have moved from God's intentions.

Let's not miss the huge difference between Paul's diagnosis of what's wrong and the world's self-evaluation. The world believes that it's so enlightened. It's high noon! But Paul knows it's midnight. We're advanced in our ability to store information on a chip and our modems are faster, but we're not necessarily getting along any better in our relationships!

For the things that have gone wrong, the world has many excuses:. "It isn't my fault." If we can't blame our parents, then maybe the genome project will free us from responsibility: "The DNA made me do it!" But for Paul, "people are without excuse" (1:20).

So what is our need? The world thinks the primary need is more knowledge of self—more self-awareness, more exploration of our inner child. But Paul knows that, while knowledge of self *can* be important and helpful, knowledge of God is what's missing.

### Daylight

Here it is, then: midnight in the garden of evil. The critical question is, How will it ever be daylight again?

One thing we know for sure. It won't happen by human insight. Our clocks are blinking 12:00 midnight.

It takes an unbelievable act of grace by the God of creation. Only he, the Creator, can intervene and also be the Redeemer.

"The people walking in darkness have seen a great light; on those living in the land of the shadow of death a light has dawned" (Isa 9:2).

"And you, my child, will be called a prophet of the Most High; for you will go on before the Lord to prepare the way for him, to give his people the knowledge of salvation through the forgiveness of their sins, because of the tender mercy of our God, by which the rising sun will come to us from heaven to shine on those living in darkness and in the shadow of death, to guide our feet into the path of peace" (Luke 1:76-79).

And one final word from the apostle Paul: "Wake up, O sleeper, rise from the dead, and Christ will shine on you!" (Eph 5:14)

### In the Light—Together

How's this for a call to unity? "Are we any better?" Paul will eventually ask (Rom 3:9). Society's dividing walls come tumbling down before such a passage. One gender can't accuse the other. One race can't point a finger at others. One generation can't claim an exemption. We all—male and female, black and white, old and young, hand-raisers and liturgy-sayers—are sinners before the living God. We live only by the gracious intervention of God through Jesus Christ.

Who is there in this church that you just can't accept? What person can't you tolerate? Whose eye has a beam protruding that drives you crazy?

Before you write them off, remember your own spiritual blindness. Remember that light has come only through the gospel—the gospel which God has generously shared with us all.

"I once was lost, but now I'm found; was blind, but now I see"—maybe it's a song we can sing in unison, with one heart and mouth as we glorify the God and Father of our Lord Jesus Christ.

## *Romans 2:12-3:20*
## *Introductory Comments*

Stephen Farris, in Chapter Four, refers to a sign put up by a church near his house that reads: "Improvement begins with 'I.'" He correctly comments, "A society addicted to self-help remedies might not welcome a word that reminds us that Christ died for the helpless."

In this message, I attempted to underscore this helplessness, this inability to save ourselves, through images of sinking ships and leaping teens. I tried to hint at my own story—as one steeped in Scripture and surrounded by religious symbols—suggesting that I could identify with those who might think we're helpless, but not nearly so helpless and desperate as those who came from the "outside."

The goal of the message is to help listeners realize that we are all on the same playing field—in need of the same gospel. In terms of responsibility, some have an advantage. But in terms of salvation, we have the same need (and, therefore, can with one heart and voice thank the God who redeemed us).

## *"No One Can Touch the Stars"*
## *Romans 2:12-3:20*

*Father, we give you thanks this morning for your gracious deliverance of us through Christ. For some of us, it was a dramatic deliverance. For others, it was more gradual, less obvious. But keep us from foolishly believing that we didn't need your rescuing hand. Please pour through me this morning the gift of preaching that we might see our common need and the unmerited gift of mercy we share through Christ, Amen.*

I'd like to ask you to carry two images in your minds as we enter the world of this morning's text. First, picture two vessels sinking out on the ocean. One is an 18-foot whaler. The other is a majestic ocean liner with a sauna, a jogging track, three work-out rooms, half a dozen pools, and enough gourmet food to feed China. There's quite a difference between these two vessels. But they have this in common: they're both sinking!

Next I'd like you to add the picture of two young men trying to touch the stars. One of them is at sea level, standing on the beach with the saltwater lapping over his toes. The other is standing on top of Mount Everest. Both are reaching, stretching with all their might, trying to touch the stars. The one who's 29,000 feet higher seems to have a distinct advantage. He is, after all, six miles closer. But isn't his effort just as futile?

At the end of our previous text, Paul made the claim that God doesn't show favoritism (2:11). But is that really true? Don't the Jews have a distinct advantage? Aren't the Gentiles having to play with one hand tied behind their backs?

It's a critical question for Paul to address. He's trying to lay a platform for unity among the believers in Rome. The big pay-off will come later in the book when he encourages the Christians to "accept one another just as Christ accepted you, in order to bring praise to God" (15:7). He desires this unity "so that with one heart and mouth [they] may glorify the God and Father of our Lord Jesus Christ" (15:6).

But this is the spade work that must be done before getting there. Don't some of us have an advantage before God? We aren't really here on the same terms, are we?

So the question before us is, do the Jews have an advantage? And Paul's answer is an unequivocal NO... and YES.

### An Advantage? No!

In terms of security, there is no advantage. Paul levels the field a bit in verses 12-16 by showing that the Gentiles have access to the law written on their hearts. It wasn't as if God didn't care about anyone but the Jews! Not only that, but the Jews didn't keep the law anyway. "It is those who obey the law who will be declared righteous."

In the next paragraph, he anticipates the rebuttal from Jewish believers. Don't they have evidence of holding the inside track to God's heart and God's judgment? What about the law? What about knowing his will and being instructed by the Torah? What about being guides for the blind? What about being lights—hadn't God said they were to be a light for the nations? What about being instructors for the foolish and teachers of children?

Our capacity for self-delusion is great. Paul points out that they had been breaking the instructions of God—

all the while claiming to be righteous and privileged (vv. 21-24). "You who preach against stealing, do you steal? You who say that people should not commit adultery, do you commit adultery? You who abhor idols, do you rob temples? You who brag about the law, do you dishonor God by breaking the law?"

Then Paul comes to the most delicate part. "The Jews don't have an advantage, huh? Then what about circumcision? Doesn't it prove that we are God's people? Isn't it the special sign of the covenant?" And Paul's answer, a bold claim, is NO! Being a person of God isn't primarily about *externals* but about the heart. Circumcision is important, for sure. It marks a person's place among the people of Israel. But of greater importance is what it points to: circumcision of the heart. "A man is a Jew if he is one inwardly; and circumcision is circumcision of the heart, by the Spirit, not by the written code."

I can just hear it now: "Paul doesn't believe in circumcision." But of course that charge couldn't stick. He saw the value of circumcision. But he knew it wasn't the one true, essential mark of walking with God. A focus on externals can get you the applause of people. It can bring a lot of self-congratulations and a lot of pride. But God's applause comes for transformed and transplanted hearts. So...no, the Jews don't have an advantage.

### An Advantage? Well, Yes!

But on the other hand...they do have an advantage. Not in terms of security, but in terms of responsibility. "What advantage, then, is there in being a Jew, or what value is there in circumcision? Much in every way!" For they had been entrusted with the very words of God.

Even the faithlessness on the part of many Jews didn't discount what God's intentions for Israel had been.

The conclusion of this section comes in 3:9. Is one group any better than the other? "Not at all! ...Jews and Gentiles alike are all under sin." Then with a series of passages from the Old Testament, Paul shows how the whole person is caught up in depravity (3:9-18): the throat, the tongue, the lips, the mouth, the feet, the eyes!

Now back to those first images. The Gentile believer may have come to Christ looking like a small whaler, while the synagogue-attending, Torah-memorizing, circumcised Jew may have coming looking like a luxury liner. But both were sinking! "There is no one righteous, not even one!"

### Don't I Have an Inside Track?

It's fairly easy for me to deal with what Paul said to the Jews. But it gets stickier when I think about what he might say to me and to this church. Do I really have no advantage? I was baptized when I was fairly young. I had a big black King James Bible full of stars for memorizing Bible verses. I knew the books of the Bible, the twelve apostles, and where Paul went on his three missionary journeys. As I recall, I was a little Bible knowledge terror.

Does it ever strike you that you may be on the inside track? You've kept your marriage together while others have given up. You've been to church your whole life. You haven't ever committed any of the "biggies."

But the apostle Paul takes the wind out of our prideful sails. We, like all others, were sinking without Christ. For it isn't so much knowledge of God's Bible that matters as it is knowledge of the God of the Bible. It isn't just immersion in water, but immersion in the heart-transforming, mind-altering, life-changing Spirit of God.

By the way, he's not telling us anything he didn't have to learn for himself. As he wrote to the Philippians, he had lots of reasons to put confidence in himself. He was "circumcised on the eighth day, of the people of Israel, of the tribe of Benjamin, a Hebrew of Hebrews; in regard to the law, a Pharisee; as for zeal, persecuting the church; as for legalistic righteousness, faultless" (Phil 3:5f). But now from his new perspective, he's able to look back and see how vain that confidence was. He said,

> Whatever was to my profit I now consider loss for the sake of Christ. What is more, I consider everything a loss compared to the surpassing greatness of knowing Christ Jesus my Lord, for whose sake I have lost all things. I consider them rubbish, that I may gain Christ and be found in him, not having a righteousness of my own that comes from the law, but that which is through faith in Christ—the righteousness that comes from God and is by faith. (Phil 3:7-9)

### A Level Playing Field

Now, back to the central theme of Romans. How does this forceful text help us live in unity and harmony with one another?

It levels the playing field. It reminds us that we're more alike than we might have thought. We might have different personalities that clash at times. We might bump and jar over what worship should look like. We might disappoint one another often. But this we have in common:

none of us can touch the stars. Some of us appear to jump a little higher than others, but compared to the height of the heavens, it's a pitifully small difference.

As Paul will say in next week's text, "There is no difference, for all have sinned and fall short." Jump as high as you want. You still fall short.

But the good news is that there's something else we all have in common here. Despite our failures to jump high enough, God has delivered us. "There is no difference, for all have sinned and fall short of the glory of God, and are justified freely by his grace through the redemption that came by Christ Jesus."

## *Romans 3:21-31*
## *Introductory Comments*

Mark Love's suggestion that the ultimate goal of preaching isn't to move from text to sermon but to allow the gospel to be in conversation with culture and Scripture is a most helpful one. In this sermon, I attempted to spark such a conversation. We're so accustomed to hearing of "amazing grace" that we've forgotten how bittersweet grace really is. For if it's offered to me—well, that's nice. But if it's offered to YOU—with all your sins, your quirks, your differences—then that's a problem. I've suggested in this sermon that not everyone who reads Romans 3:21-31 begins dancing with joy.

But as we seek to re-create the scandal of the message—a message which ultimately allowed Jewish believers and Gentile believers to glorify God with one heart and voice (15:6), we get to hear the Paul who is not so much a preacher of texts as a proclaimer of the gospel of Christ.

## "The Little Engine That Couldn't"
## Romans 3:21-31

*Lord, we love the message of your grace. We love to hear how WE have been delivered and how WE have been re-formed through Christ. But the message is sometimes dangerous, for it feels out of control. Please pour through me today the gift of preaching as we hear again the true scandal of this grace—and may this truth of Scripture knit us together as fellow-believers who with one heart and mouth glorify you, the God and father of our Lord Jesus Christ, through whom we pray, Amen.*

Everyone knows the little engine that could. It is stamped into our American psyche. While it may not be as theologically deep as some of my favorite children's books (like *Green Eggs and Ham*, and *Go, Dog, Go*), it is a powerful story that calls for perseverance.

But there's a downside to Christ-followers taking that story too far. One problem is that it may encourage self-congratulations that aren't appropriate. It took a lot of effort, but we got up that hill! High fives all around! Others gave up; some got on the wrong theological track; but *we kept going*. We thought we could, we thought we could, we thought we could—and we did!

A second problem is that it may encourage us to keep others out of our little winners' circle. If you can't shovel coal fast enough, you don't climb the hill. This makes sure we don't wind up with too many trains on top of the hill. Imagine how crowded and inconvenient that could be!

A "little-engine-that-could" myth seems to lie behind the divisions in the church in Rome. You recall that Paul writes to remind them that the gospel is for ALL—to the Jew first, but also for the Gentiles. Same gospel, same church.

After a dramatic portrayal of the spiritual darkness all around—darkness within those who didn't grow up with Torah and also within those who did!—he concludes: "There is no difference, for all have sinned and fall short of the glory of God" (3:22-23). I think Paul would prefer Shel Silverstein's take on "the little engine that could":

> *The little blue engine looked up at the hill.*
> *His light was weak, his whistle was shrill.*
> *He was tired and small, and the hill was tall,*
> *And his face blushed red as he softly said,*
> *"I think I can, I think I can, I think I can."*
>
> *So he started up with a chug and a strain,*
> *And he puffed and pulled with might and main.*
> *And slowly he climbed, a foot at a time,*
> *And his engine coughed as he whispered soft,*
> *"I think I can, I think I can, I think I can."*
>
> *With a squeak and a creak and a toot and a sigh,*
> *With an extra hope and an extra try,*
> *He would not stop—now he neared the top—*
> *And strong and proud he cried out loud,*
> *"I think I can, I think I can, I think I can."*
>
> *He was almost there, when—CRASH!*
>    *SMASH! BASH!*
> *He slid down and mashed into engine hash*
> *On the rocks below...which goes to show*

*If the track is tough and the hill is rough,*
*THINKING you can just ain't enough!*

This is much better theology. Every one of us is a wreck! It doesn't matter if we're an old, worn-out, coal-burning engine or a brand new Amtrak. We have been derailed!

Jews and Gentiles are in the same condition—even if some managed to creep half-way up the hill. Those of us who grew up going to church, attending Vacation Bible School, and memorizing Bible verses are in the same place as those who never heard the name Jesus. "All have sinned and fall short...."

**But Now**

The dramatic intervention of God to help all us wrecks is introduced with the words "but now." "But now a righteousness from God, apart from law, has been made known, to which the Law and the Prophets testify" (3:21). If the hill represents salvation, then we got there because God picked us up and airlifted us there. It's a gift of his grace.

In this paragraph, Paul pulls out several word pictures to help us, in the blindness of our spiritual pride, to see. First, we have been "justified" (v. 24). This word from the courtroom reminds us that God has declared us to be righteous. Jesus was perfectly, morally righteous. Because he took our penalty, God declares us to be righteous when we put our trust in him.

Second, we have been "redeemed" (v. 24)—a word from the marketplace. We were slaves to sin, so God provided the ransom himself by sending his own Son. We, therefore, are set free.

A third word picture comes from the altar. Christ was a "sacrifice of atonement" (v. 25). Because our sins have separated us from God, he sent his Son as our atoning Passover Lamb. Sin has therefore been removed. As John Stott has said, "The essence of our problem is man substituting himself for God, while the essence of salvation is God substituting himself for man."

Keep in mind that the burning question behind Romans isn't "How can a person riddled with guilt find release from that guilt?" Rather, it is "How can we have a community made up of both Jews and Gentiles?"

In this text, we see a movement toward unity through two responses. First, people are the same. All have participated in this rebellion against God. We've all been derailed along the tracks.

Second, God is one (v. 30). He has offered his grace to everyone, showing no favoritism. Whether you're wrecked at the very bottom of the hill or half-way up, God will rescue you.

And here is the scandal of our text. A true insider is someone with trust in Christ. Not someone with great trust. Not someone with a well-focused trust. Just trust. You come into relationship with God, not through law-keeping or better Bible study skills or spiritual pedigree, but through trust in Jesus.

### Amazing Grace—How Bittersweet the Sound

That sounds like great news if you come to Romans asking Martin Luther's question about finding release from guilt. But it's a bit offensive when you're asking Paul's question about building a united community. It means that God is showing grace to the *other* guy!

We love God's amazing grace for people like us: people who are relatively(!) moral, who read and interpret Scripture carefully, who worship regularly, who pay off our credit cards, who participate in United Way, and who see the dentist regularly.

But when God starts extending that grace generously to others, it's a bittersweet grace. Call it the dark side of grace.

Don't think that everyone in the church in Rome received this declaration with joy. "Hey, guess what! We heard from Paul. And we're saved by grace!" No, some were shaking their heads. You know where such teaching leads.

We're so used to hearing the good news of grace that we've forgotten the bad news of grace.

Remember the story Jesus told about the workers in the field (Matthew 20)? It was great news for those who showed up right before everyone punched out for the day. But what kind of news was it for those who'd been downing Gatorade all day just to keep from dehydrating? "These men who were hired last worked only one hour and you have made them equal to us who have borne the burden of the work and the heat of the day."

Or what about the story he told of the younger brother who selfishly left home and wound up feeding pigs? We've learned to bash the elder brother, but don't you think his complaint has some validity? "Look! All these years I've been slaving for you and never disobeyed your orders. Yet you never gave me even a young goat so I could celebrate with my friends. But when this son of yours, who has squandered your property with prostitutes comes home, you kill the fattened calf for him!" He's got a point, you know. What's it going to teach our middle schoolers if they see us throw parties for prodigals?

This is the dark side of grace. It's not the shiny medal awarded for me for climbing the hill. It's a medal given graciously by God to those who are in Christ.

### Reclaimed Wrecks

But herein is the good news. For in moments of spiritual insight, we can see that we aren't shiny new Amtraks but wrecks who have been salvaged and reshaped by God in Christ.

And that other person? That person with bad politics, quirky ideas, a different worship preference, and a deficient theology? Because of God's gift and through their simple trust in Christ, they journey on the same tracks you travel on.

And as we chug along, our theme isn't "I think I can, I think I can, I think I can," but rather "I know God has, I know God has, I know God has." It's our theme song of redemption as we glorify the God and Father of our Lord Jesus Christ with one heart and one mouth.

## Romans 6:1-14
## Introductory Comments

"We preachers often seem to suffer from a compulsion to tell people what to do." These words from Stephen Farris resonate with me. I think I was born a moralizer (my parents can, I believe, confirm this). It's so easy to flatten the contours of Scripture—narrative, psalms, epistles, parables—so that everything becomes another message on "Keys to Communication," "Steps to Leadership," or "Avenues to Purity."

Romans 6:1-14 is a text with some imperatives, to be sure. But even here, Paul gets at the imperatives by reminding the believers of the indicatives, as both James Walters and Dave Bland emphasize in their chapters. Paul jogs their memories, urging them to grasp the radical implications of baptism.

I challenged the members of my congregation to commit to holy, obedient lives by reminding them of their own baptisms, and what God did for them then and there. "Think back for just a moment about your baptism .... Can you maybe even feel the water on your cheeks as you came out? Do you remember the feeling of being fresh, clean, and new? It's a one-time event. But it marked you forever."

## "Leave It There"
## Romans 6:1-14

*Lord, give us keen memories today to remember the cleansing flood of baptism. Please pour through me the gift of preaching that we might clearly see our new identities as children of yours—dead to sin, but alive to Christ, through whom we pray, Amen.*

*"What shall we say, then? Shall we go on sinning so that grace may abound?"*

Can you imagine someone actually asking that? I guess it's possible. But much more likely is that people who were miffed at Paul's words were anticipating the danger ahead by predicting what others might say.

"Grace, huh, Paul? Do you know where that's going to lead? Can you imagine the immorality that will fill our churches? Can you imagine what will happen to the thinking and behavior of our teenagers?"

If you want to make religious people mad, preach the gospel of grace. Announce that all of us in the body of Christ—old-timers and newcomers, married, single, and divorced, those with a religious heritage and those without one—are forgiven by God's grace. *Not* because of our good works, *not* because we got our lives polished and buffed, but because God graciously received us in Christ.

Some are nervous about unadulterated grace because of pride. Can people who've lived ungodly lives be accepted on the same terms as those of us who grew up singing "Jesus Loves Me"? And others are nervous about the message because of fear. What's going to happen to the lives of people if we tell them they're saved by grace alone through faith alone in Christ alone? Will, for example, a brother or sister in a troubled marriage be willing to continue struggling to make the relationship work? Or have we made it too easy for them to bail?

Despite these naysayers, Paul refuses to budge on his message. But if they think his message leads to moral laxity, they haven't listened carefully. More exactly, they have failed to understand what happened to them. They have moved from the realm of Adam to the realm of Christ. Everything is now new. "We died to sin; how can we live in it any longer?"

## Baptismal Memory

To argue this, he takes them back to their baptisms. There in the water is the truth of their new identity. To wonder if grace leads to bad behavior is to fail to understand the radical act of baptism.

So what exactly happened there? We were united with Christ. We were born into Adam; but in baptism we were born again into Christ. It is the place where God did something. Baptism isn't a human work in which we can take pride. It is a testimony to our desperate need. Have you ever noticed the passive language involved? "We were baptized." "We were buried with him." "We were crucified." Not much to brag about there—except in what God has done!

What a powerful statement! When we are immersed, we re-enact the central saving event: the death, burial, and resurrection of Jesus.

But Paul wants to be sure we know this isn't just the *end* of something (the old life). It is also the *beginning* of something (new life in Christ). A new person comes up out of the water, filled with the Spirit. And from that moment on, sin is renounced! A sin-dominated life is unthinkable. That wouldn't fit our new identity. It would be like having a baby born, celebrating the birth, and then acting like future growth and care were unimportant.

### Galekeyo

In baptism, we left something behind: our attachment to sin. Right after my older son's baptism, he received an e-mail from an older friend who is a missionary in Uganda. His friend wrote:

> We have a saying here in Uganda when someone comes back from a funeral. (That happens a lot here. People die every day thanks to AIDS.) They always say to each other, '*Galekeyo.*' One day we asked what it meant and a man said in English it means 'leave it there.' In other words, all the sorrow and worries and memories should be left in the grave. We now say '*galekeyo*' when people are baptized and it really hits home with them.

Have you ever caught yourself treating your moral failures lightly because you knew God would forgive you anyway? Does your belief in grace make you less committed to make your marriage work? or less committed to the little obligations of church life? or less determined to resist the temptations of sin? Then you've misunderstood God's transforming grace. He not only forgives sin; he also delivers us from domination by sin. We'll still make mistakes. No one reaches perfection in this life. But we *galekeyo*; we leave our mistakes there. But we don't have to be moral jellyfish, drifting around at the mercy of the wind and waves.

A former mistress passed Augustine after his conversion, turned around after he didn't acknowledge her, and said, "Augustine, it is I." "Yes," he's supposed to have replied, "but it is no longer I." How true. We've been crucified with Christ, and we no longer live. But Christ lives in us (Galatians 2:20).

A life of sin just doesn't fit our baptismal identity. We have been buried with Christ. We've been clothed with Christ. As Paul asks about sin, "How can we live in it any longer?"

In the graphic language of verse 7, we have been freed from the dominion of sin. Prisoners who've been freed shouldn't return to their prison cell, though some do. After all, after so many years that cell has become familiar territory. It comes with three square meals a day. It has come to be home.

But we've been given a new home. Baptism was both a funeral and a resurrection. We died to the old life of sin; we were raised to walk new lives in Jesus.

### Dead to Sin, Alive to God

There are a couple of implications from this truth. First, **we must not downplay sin**. We must never act like it isn't important because we've been forgiven anyway. Let's not identify with W. H. Auden, when he wrote, "Every crook will argue: 'I like committing crimes. God likes forgiving them. Really the world is admirably arranged.'"

We must fight against sinful values and behavior with every fiber of our being, knowing that the real power in the battle comes from the Holy Spirit. We're not under the dictatorship of sin any longer, but it won't leave us alone. So we battle. As Larry Crabb has said:

> *The disguise must be ripped away, the horror of the enemy's ugliness and the pain he creates must be seen, not to understand the ugliness, not to endlessly study the pain, but to shoot the enemy.*
>
> *And if he doesn't stay dead, we must shoot him again, then beat him, then tie him down in the sand under a hot desert sun, turn loose an army of red ants on his body and walk away without sympathy. And then we must do it again and again and again, till we're home. An overdone metaphor? Not when we see the enemy for who he is, for what he wants to do. We are at war, the enemy within is the flesh, and he wants to ruin our relationships and thwart God's plan. If we don't hate the enemy, we'll hate something or someone else.*

What do you maybe need to relinquish today? What pet sin have you been allowing to remain? In Scripture, sin is described as leaving the path, as missing the mark, as straying from the fold. In light of this text, it doesn't fit your new identity that began in the waters of baptism. That raging anger, that uncontrolled materialism, that seething prejudice, that hidden lust—they just don't match your new baptismal identity.

A second implication, however, is that **we must not become obsessed with sin.** For the real battle isn't to get rid of sin; the real battle is to glorify God, to worship him, to experience his presence, to enjoy hearing his voice, and to trust him in everything.

Philip Yancey has written about a summer when he had to learn German to finish his graduate degree. What a horrible summer. His friends were sailing on Lake Michigan, riding bikes, and having fun while he was stumbling through German nouns and verbs. And it was a perfunctory task for only one purpose: to get his degree.

Later he wondered: What could have made this experience of learning different?

> If my wife, the woman I fell in love with, spoke only German, I would have learned the language in record time....I would have stayed up late at night parsing verbs and placing them properly at the ends of my love-letter sentences, treasuring each addition to my vocabulary as a new way of expressing myself to the one I loved. I would have learned German unbegrudgingly, with the relationship itself as my reward.

There's a stern tone in part of this morning's text. This tone calls us away from lives that flirt with sin. "We died to sin; how can we live in it any longer?" "Anyone who has died has been freed from sin." "Count yourselves dead to sin." "Do not let sin reign in your mortal body so that you obey its evil desires." "Do not offer the parts of your body to sin."

But behind that stern tone is the loving voice of a God who loves us deeply. He knows how sin can wreck lives. And the deepest invitation in the text is to celebrate life in him. "Count yourselves dead to sin but ALIVE TO GOD in Christ Jesus." "Do not offer the parts of your body to sin...rather OFFER YOURSELVES TO GOD, as those who have been brought from death to life."

Think back for just a moment about your baptism. Can you remember the ridiculous clothes you wore? Can you see the faces of those who were watching? Can you maybe even feel the water on your cheeks as you came out? Do you remember the feeling of being fresh, clean, and new?

It's a one-time event. But it marked you forever. So, Galekeyo. Leave it there. And go live the new life in Christ!

## *Romans 8:1-17*
## *Introductory Comments*

As James Walters explains in his contribution to this book, the framework for understanding Romans 8 comes from the discussion of the two dominions (Adam and Christ) in chapter 5. Here in 8:1-17, as Walters points out, "Paul explains how the Holy Spirit assists believers in their continuing struggle with sin."

I hoped to underscore both our inability to break free from sin by trying harder and the power to put "to death the deeds of the body" through God's indwelling Spirit through the wonderful images of Ezekiel 37. Dead bones can't come to life through education, encouragement, or 24/7 effort! Only God's Spirit can enliven them.

## *"The Divine Invasion"*
## *Romans 8:1-17*

*O Lord, please pour through me today the gift of preaching that this word that spoke so eloquently to the church in Rome might speak to us at Highland again this morning. Open our hearts to the cleansing, sanctifying work of your Spirit, as we pray through Christ—the one who has set us free!—Amen.*

I would have loved to have seen that valley that Ezekiel saw when he was led out by the Spirit of the Lord. A valley full of bones. Ezekiel said: "[The Lord] led me back and forth among them, and I saw a great many bones on the floor of the valley, bones that were very dry" (Ezekiel 37:2).

How would you like to have been put on the church committee that was in charge of making those bones come to life? How would you try to pull that off?

I'm sure some learned person on the committee would suggest that we educate those bones. This would be the same person who thinks that education and more teaching is the answer to everything: giving, evangelism, healthy marriages, etc.

Someone else might recommend a good tongue-lashing. Just pile on the guilt. Make them work harder—until they're bone tired.

And then, of course, there would be the committee cheerleader: someone who thinks the bones just need a big dose of encouragement and affirmation. Maybe they need a good pep talk like George C. Scott at the beginning of "Patton." Maybe they need a locker room "win-one-for-the-Gipper" speech. Maybe the group could sit around and sing for them: "The hip bone connected to the thigh bone...."

But after all the teaching, all the guilt, and all the encouragement, the valley would still be filled with dry, lifeless bones.

The good news of the gospel begins in bad news: we are not up to the task. We can't save ourselves, and we can't purify ourselves once we are saved. We can make decisions, we can offer ourselves to God, but we can't provide the power it takes to become God-like.

### The "God and I" Illusion

It's so easy to think that sanctification is something I do—with a little help from God. We're like the cricket that hitched a ride on the back of an elephant as it stomped across an old bridge. After they reached the other side, the cricket chirped, "We sure did make that thing shake, didn't we?"

Or I remember hearing about the night Michael Jordan scored sixty-nine points for the Bulls. That night, Stacy King, a rookie, got in the game. Afterwards, King was asked to give his reflections on the memorable evening. He said, "I'll always remember it as the night Michael Jordan and I combined to score seventy points."

We cannot, on our own resources, whip sin. And it's good news to have that bad news admitted. We don't have the power to put away old grudges, or to break addictions to internet pornography, or to save our marriages. Remember how Paul described a person who, without the Holy Spirit, is just trying harder and harder to keep the law?

For I have the desire to do what is good, but I cannot carry it out. For what I do is not the good

I want to do; no, the evil I do not want to do—
this I keep on doing. Now if I do what I do not
want to do, it is no longer I who do it, but it is
sin living in me that does it.

I believe the first step of AA is right: you must begin
by admitting that you are wholly, utterly powerless in
this battle.

We have to eventually learn what Ezekiel learned:
that those bones would not come to life by education
(teach more!), guilt (try harder!), or encouragement (just
give it another shot!).

Then [the Lord] said to me, "Prophesy to these
bones and say to them, 'Dry bones, hear the
word of the Lord! This is what the Sovereign
Lord says to these bones: I will make breath enter
you, and you will come to life. I will attach
tendons to you and make flesh come upon you
and cover you with skin; I will put breath in you,
and you will come to life. Then you will know
that I am the Lord.

### The Invasion

In this section of Romans, Paul is urging his
brothers and sisters in Christ to live holy lives that are
commensurate with what happened at their baptisms.
They (and we!) are to resist sin with everything that's in
them. They are to avoid compromise, caving in, and
complacency. Human choice and human responsibility
are essential.

But they don't supply the power needed to become
godly! Trying harder to keep the law won't work because
sin has hijacked the law. We wind up, despite our best

intentions, doing the things we said we wouldn't do, and not doing the things we committed to doing. We are a valley of dry bones.

So how do we live holy lives? How does the church live the new life that reflects the salvation we've already received? **God sent his Son into the world to break the power of sin, and he has sent his Spirit into our hearts to help us resist the temptations of sin.**

To Paul, the Spirit's powerful presence in a person's life is the one sure mark of Christian identity. Not agape love. Not nonresistance in the face of persecution. Not humility. Not church membership. "You, however, are controlled not by the sinful nature but by the Spirit, if the Spirit of God lives in you. And if anyone does not have the Spirit of Christ, he does not belong to Christ" (8:9). The very words of God in Ezekiel turned out to be true:

> I will give you a new heart and put a new spirit in
> you; I will remove from you your heart of stone
> and give you a heart of flesh. And I will put my
> Spirit in you and move you to follow my decrees
> and be careful to keep my laws.

God is performing his surgery in our hearts through his Holy Spirit. This is the power—not our best efforts to run faster or climb higher. God has written his law on our hearts and has given us the Spirit to live in harmony with his will.

### Two Channel Markers

There are a couple of channel markers for us to observe as we hear this victorious words of Romans 8.

First, Paul isn't expecting us to be perfect. The new age of the kingdom has broken in, but it isn't here fully yet. I'm sure he'd agree with the voice of 1 John: that anyone who claims to be sinless is self-deluded or full of lies.

The second channel marker is that Paul isn't expecting us to be passive. We're not just innocent onlookers as the Spirit does his work. We are called on to walk in step with the Spirit. These powerful words are full of choices that we must make. Will we live like we belong to Adam still or like we belong to Christ?

### The Divine Infection

Just before the Italians were driven out of Eritrea, a city in North Africa, during World War II, they tried to make the valuable harbor worthless for the allies by filling large barges with concrete and sinking them across the harbor entrance.

The way those barges got moved was a bit of genius. The Allied forces took huge gas tanks and sealed them so they'd float. When the tide went out, they chained those tanks to the barges. Then when the tide flowed back in, the law of displacement took over: the tanks lifted those heavy barges. Then ships could remove them from that strategic point.

So what force lifted the barges? The chains? Not exactly. The tanks? Not really? The water? More than that. The barges were lifted by the gravitational attraction of the moon. Now that's power!

This is the way our battle with sin goes. We could yank and tug all day, but sheer effort won't win. We can't fix a broken marriage. We can't whip the onslaught of sin. But God's Spirit provides the power we need.

For those who are weary of sin's ravages, for those who have faced up to the bad news that all their attempts to try harder have failed, here is the good news to celebrate: "If the Spirit of him who raised Jesus from the dead is living in you, he who raised Christ from the dead will also give life to your mortal bodies through his Spirit, who lives in you." Dry bones can live again!

## Romans 8:18-39
## Introductory Comments

Behind this message were painful losses in our church, including two ten-year-old girls. We had prayed diligently for these children, begging God to heal them. And we had suffered through their deaths.

One of them was my daughter, Megan. So this isn't just an academic exercise in fine-tuning the "already/not yet" perspective of my church; rather, it is the hope of a grieving father.

While I've tried not to make Megan's death the center of my preaching universe, it's been amazing to see the impact when I've talked openly (sometimes much more openly than in this message) about my grief, my doubt, and my hope.

First, people tell me that they feel closer to me. They realize I'm not a homiletical machine. Second, it seems to give others permission to explore openly their own suffering and grief. And third, it allows people to see that hope shines through, right in the midst of even the greatest tragedy.

## "Waiting"
### Romans 8:18-39

*O Lord, most of our lives haven't turned out quite like we imagined they would. Detours popped up that we hadn't anticipated. Roads were closed that we thought might be open. Some have come this morning with the salt of fresh tears around their eyes. Others have smiles on the outside while the tears are in their hearts. So please pour through me today the gift of preaching that we might catch a glimpse of your continuing work of redemption and care. Move beyond my losses and my joys to the transforming gospel of Christ, in whom we pray, Amen.*

### The Difficulty of Waiting

My all-time favorite ad in a religious journal appeared several years ago in the *Christian Chronicle*. A new recording was out from the Harding A Capella Choir entitled "Teach Me Lord to Wait." Inside the advertisement was a box one could cut out to mail in an order. It said: "PLEASE RUSH ME A COPY OF 'TEACH ME LORD TO WAIT.'"

I can appreciate that. I'm not a very good wait-er, and I'm guessing most of you aren't either. Just answer this: how many of you have ever gotten in a line at the grocery store and kept track of where you would have been had you chosen a different line? Or, how many of you have filled your gas tank only halfway not because you didn't have the cash but because it was taking too long? We don't like waiting!

I can tell the children at Highland have a difficult time waiting. Sometimes an assembly will end that I thought was wonderful. People seemed to be hanging on my words, the singing was rapturous, and it felt like the roof almost opened with heaven descending. Then as I walk out I'll see some of our worship bulletins where children have marked off the items of worship one by one. (At least I choose to assume it is the children!) For them, it isn't so much about rapture as about tortuous waiting.

Did I mention before that I don't like waiting?! I don't like waiting on tests to come back for people I love. I don't like waiting on a teenager to return when there's ice on the streets. I don't like waiting outside an ICU. And I don't like waiting to see my daughter again. I don't like waiting.

Henri Nouwen said that our disdain for waiting is because it seems like a dry desert between where we are and where we want to go. It seems like a waste of time. We want to get going! We want to do something!

Unfortunately, waiting is exactly what we must do. Paul put it well: "we groan inwardly as we wait eagerly." We have already been adopted as the children of God, but we don't yet fully enjoy the full inheritance. We've already been redeemed, but not with the full redemption of our bodies. We have tasted the presence of God, but we are not yet fully in his presence like we will some day be.

At the end of his previous section, Paul transitions with the two words that carry through our text: sufferings and glory (v. 17).

### Groaning

The older you get, the more you see how fallen this world is. This isn't "The Truman Show," where everything is tweaked and controlled. We don't live in a protective bubble. In verse 35, Paul lists seven of the pins that are constantly bursting our bubbles: trouble, hardship, persecution, famine, nakedness, danger, and sword. Then he quotes from Psalm 44, a communal lament that basically cries out: "Hey, would somebody please go wake God up?"

This world is full of illness, abandonment, loss and grief, hunger, financial reverses, and death. The sooner you face these negative realities, the better off you are! We are not living in the Garden of Eden! Larry Crabb nails it when he writes:

> *Modern Christianity, in dramatic reversal of its biblical form, promises to relieve the pain of living in a fallen world. The message, whether it's from fundamentalists requiring us to live by a favored set of rules or from charismatics urging a deeper surrender to the Spirit's power, is too often the same: The promise of bliss is for now! Complete satisfaction can be ours this side of heaven.*
>
> *Some speak of the joys of fellowship and obedience, others of a rich awareness of their value and worth. The language may be reassuringly biblical or it may reflect the influence of current psychological thought. Either way, the point of living the Christian life has shifted from knowing and serving Christ till He returns to soothing, or at least learning to ignore, the ache in our soul.*
>
> *...Beneath the surface of everyone's life, especially the more mature, is an ache that will not go away. It can be ignored, disguised, mislabeled, or submerged by a torrent of activity, but it will not disappear. And for good reason. We were designed to enjoy a better world than this. And until that*

*better world comes along, we will groan for what*
*we do not have. An aching soul is evidence not of*
*neurosis or spiritual immaturity, but of realism.*

Paul uses an appropriate word to describe our current experience: groaning. God's people are groaning inwardly (v. 23), not only because of the suffering we experience but even more because of the glory that's ahead for which we wait. And it isn't just the people who are groaning; all creation is groaning (v. 22). It is aching from flooding and famine, from hurricanes and twisters, from pollution in the air and pollution in the water. Here, in three words, is Paul's commentary on Genesis 3: "bondage to decay" (v. 21).

This isn't moaning, however. It is *groaning*—which reaches forward to the glory that lies ahead. Our current suffering can't begin to compare to that glory.

### Moving Toward a Grand Conclusion

Paul anticipates the glory ahead when God liberates creation from its bondage to decay. Sin destroyed the harmony God intended in this world, but he will redeem creation, turning everything back to its original purpose. Just as he'll transform our bodies, he will transform all creation into "the new heavens and the new earth." He will reverse the effects of the fall and renew his good creation. This is a quite different picture than some of us have had of everything being annihilated. Haven't you ever wondered why Jesus said the meek will inherit the earth? ("Sure, give it to the meek. It'll be wiped out, but they won't complain!") Paul pictures not another creation, but this one redeemed, renewed, and refurbished.

He also anticipates the redemption of our bodies (v. 23). What a glorious time: no more pain, no more death, no more suffering. We will dwell in the presence of God forever!

And even now, God is moving everything inexorably in that direction. "And we know that in all things God works for the good of those who love him, who have been called according to his purpose. For those God foreknew he also predestined to be conformed to the likeness of his Son, that he might be the firstborn among many brothers. And those he predestined, he also called; those he called, he also justified; those he justified, he also glorified" (8:28-30).

Based on an inaccurate translation—"all things work together for good"—some have pinned all kinds of bad things on "the will of God." But Paul isn't telling us that everything that happens is ultimately good because it was God's will. And he isn't even telling us that God can use even bad things to produce good, though that interpretation is closer to the truth. He is making the bold claim that *God is moving history toward a grand conclusion*. The God who has known us, predestined us to be like Christ, called us, and justified us has also declared our glory—a glory that we haven't fully received yet. This is a rugged promise for people who have faced up to the aches of their soul, for people who have cried their eyes out with grief and hope.

So...caught now between the sufferings we experience and the glory we anticipate, *how* do we wait? In hope, in endurance, in confidence. *Why* do we wait? Because we have learned in Christ to trust God. We can feel the momentum building in the text as Paul now asks five questions:

(1) "If God is for us, who can be against us?" (v. 31). The answer for believers is obvious. This God who knew us, predestined us, called us, justified us, and glorified us is a God on whom we can count. He will not ultimately disappoint us.

(2) "Won't God graciously give us all things?" (v. 32). Think about it: God has already done a harder thing. He gave his Son for us when we were still sinners and enemies. He'll surely do this.

(3) "Who will bring any charge against those God has chosen?" (v. 33). No one! For God is the judge in this courtroom, and he's already ruled in our favor.

(4) "Who is he that condemns?" (v. 34). Again—no one! Jesus died, was raised, and is now interceding for us at God's right hand. There is no one who'll be able to condemn us.

(5) "Who shall separate us from the love of Christ?" (v. 35). This is where he lists those seven possibilities: trouble, hardship, persecution, famine, nakedness, danger, and the sword. But no, even "in all these things we are more than conquerors through him who loved us" (v. 37).

Christ was rejected, crowds mocked him, friends abandoned him, the Roman government nailed him to a cross, and he was laid in a tomb. But on the third day, God *raised him from the dead*. And ever since that day, suffering cannot have the final say. Nothing can separate us from the love of God that is in Christ Jesus our Lord.

### The Long Wait

Right now we wait. And as we wait, there is groaning. We **groan** under the oppression of fallenness as we wait for the glory ahead. We **long** for a day without tears, without pain, without death. We **yearn** for the fullness of God's presence which alone can satisfy our deepest longings. We **pray** with our brothers and sisters through the ages, Marana Tha!, "Come, O Lord." And we **sing**:

> *Lord, haste the day when the faith shall be sight*
> *The clouds be rolled back as a scroll.*
> *The trump shall resound and the Lord shall descend.*
> *Even so, it is well with my soul.*

I love to hear testimonies of God's miraculous intervention. But I also want the church to be honest. For every testimony about a marriage that was miraculously delivered, I want us to hear of one we prayed for that didn't make it (but where God's merciful sustenance was still evident). For every story of someone who was miraculously healed, we need to hear of someone for whom we prayed who wasn't healed but who was overwhelmed in illness and death by the unfathomable love of God.

# 7

# Sermons from Romans 9-16
### Ken Durham

## Romans 9-11
## Introductory Comments

This sermon was included in a series on Romans, preached to a university congregation on the campus of Pepperdine University in Malibu, California. Of all sections of Romans, 9-11 is probably the one most neglected by preachers. Paul here addresses the Jewish community with difficult language and argumentation, so the temptation for the expository preacher is to hopscotch over it to get to the good stuff beyond. But this is hardly dispensable material. In an epistle about salvation—how is it made possible and who will live in assurance of it—9-11 deserves more than a sermonic footnote.

In my Romans series, I included in each sermon an imagined "conversation" between Paul and two young

Christians—Adelphos and Adelphe—who have come from Rome to Corinth to question Paul about the letter he sent their church. My congregation is made up of almost one-half university students, and I wanted to encourage my young listeners to identify with the first hearers of the text, approaching Romans as the "shared constitutive narrative" Steven Farris describes.

How this worked was each week I asked different young adults, usually university students, to be my "Adelphos" and "Adelphe." They were given a script of the dialogue beforehand and were encouraged to read it conversationally. They read into a microphone from the front row of the auditorium, interacting with me, the voice of Paul. This device offers other creative communicative possibilities, such as a more dramatic and less obviously-scripted conversation between Paul and his young questioners at the podium; this would have the advantage of being more lively, but would require more rehearsal time.

I opened with *"Schindler's List"*—a salvation story with an unconventional savior—to introduce this message on God's saving purposes. The claim of this text (and sermon) is: God rejects no one who comes to him in obedient faith, so confess ("Jesus is Lord"), believe, and you will be saved.

## Before Schindler's List
## Romans 9-11

I was the first member of my group to finish the tour of the U.S. Holocaust Memorial Museum in Washington, D.C., so I went exploring. I found the research floor and an information desk, and for some reason was prompted to ask the young man there, "Say, would you by any chance happen to have a copy of Schindler's list?" "Why yes, we do," he said with some hesitation, and then, "You know, you're the first person to ask me that question." I decided to press my advantage. "I don't suppose you would make me a copy of it, would you?" "Sure," he said, and returned a few minutes later, handing me a nineteen-page photocopy of a photocopy of the list of the 1101 Jews—297 women, 804 men—employed at Oskar Schindler's enamelware factory in Cracow, Poland, during World War II.

So here it is, in my hand: Schindler's list. If you read the book by Thomas Keneally or saw the film by Steven Spielberg, you know that having your name on this list meant *salvation*. Oskar Schindler was a Nazi. And a hard-drinking philanderer. And an opportunistic businessman who made millions off the war. But by war's end he had spent every last tainted penny to secure the safety of the 1101 Jewish men and women who worked for him. He literally bought their lives from the Nazis through well-placed bribes and payoffs. Today the survivors and descendants of the *Schindlerjuden*—(Schindler's Jews) as they came to be known—number over six thousand.

### The man of constant sorrow

Romans 9-11 is about the salvation of the Jews. For years now Paul has been traveling all over the

Mediterranean world, issuing the challenge of Christ as God's specially-appointed "apostle to the Gentiles." But even though the Gentiles are his divinely-ordained assignment, his territory, whenever he first hits a town, he always goes first...to the synagogue! And predictably, painfully, he almost always gets tossed out! Most of his fellow Jews just can't see it, just can't bring themselves to accept Jesus as their long-awaited Messiah. And this just breaks Paul's heart!

Listen to Paul's anguish over the Jews. He could be singing the signature song of the recent film, "O Brother, Where Art Thou?"—"I am a man of constant sorrow."

> I have great sorrow and unceasing anguish in my heart. For I could wish that I myself were cursed and cut off from Christ for the sake of my brothers, those of my own race, the people of Israel. (Rom 9:2-4)

*"My brothers! My race!"* With this burden heavy on his heart, Paul breaks with the overall flow of his epistle and spends three chapters—Romans 9-11—wrestling with the place of the Jewish nation in God's salvation history.

Some have called this section of Romans a parenthesis, a detour from the main road, the dullest and least relevant portion of the book. (It's the part of Romans preachers often choose to skip to get on to "the good stuff" in chapter 12.) But there are those who argue that Romans 9-11 is absolutely vital to Paul's working out of his gospel. Krister Stendahl calls this section "the real center of gravity of Romans." So maybe we had best not skip it.

**The conversation**

Romans is one of the richest, deepest, densest portions of Scripture. But it was not written as a seminary textbook. It's a *letter*—carefully-reasoned and formally-composed, inspired by God—but still, a letter. A personal letter, written by a sinner, to sinners. A letter intended to be of practical use to a local church.

So with that in mind, we try to enter into its "conversation" by imagining a dialogue about our text in Romans each week. Picture two young Roman Christians—brother and sister—who have tracked Paul down in Corinth (where we think the book of Romans may have been written) to probe the meaning of his epistle to their church. We'll call them Adelphos and Adelphe, which in Greek means "brother" and "sister."

**Adelphe**: Paul, there's one section of your letter to us—a pretty lengthy section, as I recall—that I personally didn't find all that spine-tingling: it's where you go on and on (and on) about Israel, and some of their dusty old history, and their resistance to the gospel today, and all that. Excuse me, but…why should I care? I'm no Israelite. And quite honestly, why should you care? I know your ancestry is Jewish, but aren't you God's apostle to us Gentiles now?

*Paul: Well first, Adelphe, you should care because many of your Christian brothers and sisters come from the same Israelite family I come from. And you should care because that "dusty old history" is an indispensable part of God's saving work in everyone's history. You have to understand how deeply personal all this is to me. The Christian fellowship is of course my closest family circle. But I will always be a Jew; these are my people. I don't expect you to understand how much I want all Israel to be saved, but believe me when I tell you, I would surrender my very soul…I would go to* hell…*for my fellow Jews, if it meant that they might all find Christ!*

**Adelphe**: But Paul, face the facts: it's not going to happen. Israel as a nation never has…and never will…all claim the promises of God. Even though God gave them the patriarchs, and the covenants, and the Law, and the temple worship, and in time, the Messiah…and still many—most—do not believe!

*Paul: I know, Adelphe. It is a great and unrelenting heartache for me. To see how resistant so many of my people are to the purposes of God.*

**Adelphe**: Well then, if so many of the Jews have rejected God's Son, has God now rejected the Jews? And if *God* has…should *we*? (I mean, these are, after all, the people who killed our Lord Jesus.)

*Paul: No, no, God has not rejected the Jewish people. God's desire—like mine—is that all Israel might be saved. But let me caution you to be very careful there, Adelphe. I'm very concerned about a dangerous anti-Jewish, anti-Semitic spirit that can be fueled by Christians using language like "the people that killed our Lord." Some of the Jewish leaders killed our Lord. And some Roman politicians killed our Lord. And—don't ever forget—our sins killed our Lord. So please, watch your language, okay?*

**Adelphe**: Okay, message received. But, I still have some questions about what God is doing with the Jews now that we're in the New Covenant Age. Has God now rejected the Jews? And, if he no longer loves the Jews, then—pardon my being so blunt—why should we non-Jews believe you when you say, "Nothing in all creation shall separate us from the love of God that is ours in Christ Jesus"?

*Paul: Okay, let me see if I can speak to those questions. (But, be warned, this is some of that stuff you found so non-"spine-tingling.") Do you remember how at the outset of my letter I said that the gospel is "the power of God for the salvation of everyone who believes ... first for the Jew, then for the Gentiles"? From the very beginning, since sin first entered this world, God's purpose has been to make his salvation available to all peoples of the earth. But by his divine sovereignty, he chose one nation, Israel, to bless—with his patriarchs and his law and his covenant—so that in the fullness of time he might bless all nations. That's what I meant when I said that salvation came "first" to the Jews.*

**Adelphos:** Hold on. Why did God do it *that* way? That doesn't make sense to me! Why just *one* nation to bless? Why not all nations at once? And why Israel? Why not the Philistines...or the Egyptians...or the Persians? See, that's what bugs me about God: he chooses whom he chooses to choose...and we're just supposed to accept that? I'm not so sure that the sovereignty of God is all that <u>fair</u>!

*Paul: Well, my young brother, if you don't mind my saying so, who are you to second-guess the Master of the universe? Since when does the creature criticize the Creator? Does a pot say to the potter, "Hey! I wanted to be a stylish vessel, or a classy urn; how come I ended up a crummy soup bowl?"*

**Adelphos:** I'm...not...a pot!

*Paul: No, you're not. You're a lump of clay, fashioned entirely by the hand of God, in the image of God, quickened by the breath of God. And you're absolutely right: God chooses whom God chooses to choose...because God is God. Almighty, all-knowing, sovereign God. "Sovereignty," I realize, is not always an easy explanation to hear...maybe*

*because we so often associate "sovereignty" with "tyranny."*
*(I don't have to tell a man who lives in Rome how that*
*works.) We don't trust rulers with absolute power because, as*
*they say, absolute power corrupts absolutely.*

*But this Ruler is God we're talking about, our*
*gracious, incorruptible Abba Father. His sovereignty is*
*tempered by his mercy. If he's unfair, then you can pretty*
*much assume that his unfairness will work in our favor, not*
*against us. And if his ways don't always make sense to you*
*...well then, maybe it's possible that the Almighty has*
*purposes or designs that you—as wise and insightful as you*
*are—can't fully see.*

*Now then ...where was I? Okay. Of all nations of the*
*earth, God chose to choose...Israel. Unimpressive,*
*stumbling, bumbling Israel. Heroic, noble, zealous Israel.*
*Obstinate, disobedient, fickle Israel. My people, Israel. To tell*
*our story is to tell of the full breadth of God's nature—his*
*grace and his wrath, his sternness and his kindness, his*
*inclusivity and his exclusivity. But when Messiah came—*
*Jesus Christ our Lord—he who was given as our cornerstone*
*became for many of the Jews a stumbling block (just as*
*Isaiah said would happen). They just couldn't, or wouldn't,*
*accept Jesus as the righteousness of God; they turned away.*
*Now, it's Gentiles like you and your sister who are walking*
*in the door of the household of God that so many Jews are*
*walking out of. My most earnest hope is that, as more and*
*more of you Gentiles come into the family of God, my Jewish*
*kinfolk will see God at work among you, see what they're*
*missing, and want to get in on it.*

*Has God rejected the Jewish people? No way. That*
*kingdom doorway is still open. God's salvation is still*
*available to all Israel. Don't ever count the Jews out! God is*
*not through with the Jews. As Brother Peter likes to say, God*
*does not will lostness for anyone, but salvation for everyone*
*(2 Pet 3:9).*

**Adelphos**: Paul, I have to tell you...I just don't understand this loyalty and devotion you have to your fellow Jews. How do you do it? How can you continue to take the gospel into their synagogues? What kind of masochist are you, to keep reaching out to these people...when you yourself are the target of so many of these anti-Christian Jewish Zealots? I mean, come on, Paul—they *expelled* you from Pisidia...they tried to *stone* you in Iconium...they *did* stone you and leave you for dead in Lystra...they forced you to *flee* Thessalonica.... Do you see a pattern here?

*Paul: Adelphos, I'm not about to allow some militant minority turn me against my own people or quiet my proclamation of the good news! I'll say it again: the gospel we preach is the power of God unto salvation! There is so much confusion and loneliness and lostness out there, Adelphos. How will that ever change, unless men and women of faith begin to act like men and women of faith? And where will faith come from...how will people know what to believe in...unless the Word of Christ is faithfully preached?*

*See these feet? Not a pretty sight, are they? But these knotty, gnarly things have covered the length and breadth of this Empire, carrying gospel wherever I can get a hearing. And Isaiah says, these are pretty good-looking feet...if they bring good news, and peace, and the joy of God's salvation* (Isa 52:7-10).

*So that's my mission — to preach the Word, to Jew and Gentile alike. As straightforwardly and unambiguously as I can. Sure, some will just shrug and walk away from it. Some will stumble over it and reject the message outright. And some will even try to silence the messenger any way they can. But some...some will be like that topsoil the Master described, receptive and teachable. So God's word, like a fertile seed, finds its way to the innermost place of a person's being, and before you know it, faith bursts forth! "Jesus is Lord!" confess the lips. "He is risen!" affirms the heart. "And you are saved!" says the God of glory.*

*O my children! What a God we have! How deep and rich and perceptive his wisdom! Don't you love discussing his mysteries like we have today? What an exhilarating challenge, to seek out a better understanding of the purposes of God! But...will we ever fully understand his will and his ways? Of course we won't! We're in way over our heads, we are way out of our league...when we try to get our minds around the mind of the Almighty, when we imagine we're smart enough to tell God what to do, when we think we could ever put him in our debt. That's why we need to love him with all our minds...and ask...and seek...and knock...and when all else is said and done, we say: He and he alone is Creator. He is Sustainer. He is Sovereign. He is Everything. To God be the glory! Amen!*

### Are you saved?

Have you ever had to be saved? Rescued? Gotten out of a fix you got yourself into and couldn't get yourself out of? It's such an embarrassing thing.

I recall a snowy winter's day in Kentucky when I came out of a convenience store and saw a woman spinning her car wheels on the ice in the parking lot. She was gunning her engine, but she wasn't going anywhere. I got behind her car and began to push. Nothing. Another guy joined me to push. Then another, and another. Soon there were five of us pushing, and she was just spinning her wheels, going nowhere. Then somebody thought to ask, "Lady, is your emergency brake on?" As she took off, she didn't even look back to say thanks. I think she was embarrassed.

Salvation. It's our greatest need, our highest hope. And yet for many people—Christians included—it's a word that makes us cringe. I heard a minister tell of the time he was sitting in a movie theater when a guy walked up and asked, "Is this seat saved?" Seizing the day, the minister responded, "No...but I am!" He said the guy went and sat somewhere else. (I don't blame him.)

Or take Ed Goforth's experience. One day Ed was walking across the campus of the University of Texas in Austin when some guy he'd never seen before jumped out from behind a shrub and shouted in his face, "Are you saved?!" Ed was pretty shaken by that bizarre bit of guerilla evangelism. He didn't find the methodology particularly attractive...but he couldn't get the question out of his head. Not long after that he showed up at our student center, started studying the Bible, was eventually baptized into Christ, and became one of the finest student leaders in our campus ministry.

"Are you saved?" It's a stark question, I know, a very personal question. It's the question from which we can never quite get away. Because we are moral creatures, by nature, you and I. We know deep down that we are responsible for our words and our deeds and our choices. We know, like Paul knew, that we are sinners, and that something or somebody is going to have to deal with the sin problem in our lives. And we can no more save ourselves, someone said, than we can pick ourselves up by our own hair.

### Saving faith

Paul never stopped worrying about the fate of his fellow Jews. Every time he got thrown out of another synagogue, I suspect he experienced that old familiar pain all over again. I don't know what to make of his statement in 11:26 that *"all Israel will be saved."* Did he mean all Jews? A remnant of the Jews? The New Israel? I don't know. But there is something here that seems crystal-clear to me. Listen.

> But what does [Scripture] say? "The word is near you; it is in your mouth and in your heart," that is, the word of faith we are proclaiming: That if you confess with your mouth, "Jesus is Lord," and believe in your heart that God raised him from the dead, you will be saved. (Rom 10:8-9)

*"What must I do to be saved?"* That's the question the Philippian jailer asked in Acts 16:30. *"Believe in the Lord Jesus, and you will be saved."* And that's the answer Paul gave in Acts 16:31. I might put in a good word here about baptism as that act of faith that connects us profoundly to the cross-event. But here—and throughout Romans—Paul focuses on FAITH as our foremost, indispensable response to God.

"The gospel…is the power of God for the salvation of all who believe" (Rom 1:16).

"[God is] the one who justifies those who have faith in Jesus" (Rom 3:26).

"God will credit righteousness—for us who believe in him who raised Jesus our Lord from the dead" (Rom 4:24).

"If you confess with your mouth, 'Jesus is Lord,' and believe in your heart that God raised him from the dead, you will be saved" (Rom 10:9).

What God wants most of all, Paul says, is our <u>trust</u>. Trust enough to say, *"Jesus is Lord,"* and mean it enough to make his Son the Master, the Boss, the C.E.O. of all our affairs. We may not understand just what kind of pot the Potter seems to be making of us, but we can surely trust his steadfast love. We shouldn't expect to fathom all his mysterious ways, but we can surely trust his righteous will.

> Oh, the depth of the riches of the wisdom and knowledge of God! How unsearchable his judgments, and his paths beyond tracing out! Who has known the mind of the Lord? Or who has been his counselor? Who has ever given to God, that God should repay him? For from him and through him and to him are all things. To him be the glory forever! Amen. (Rom 11:33-36)

As the film "Schindler's List" comes to a close, Oskar Schindler's Jewish workers gather at midnight to say goodbye to the man who saved them from the ovens. Germany has surrendered to the Allies and Schindler, a Nazi, must flee. They present him with a parting gift, a ring, made from the gold of a grateful survivor's tooth. It is inscribed with a verse from the Talmud: "He who saves a single life saves the entire world."

Oskar Schindler's list saved 1101 men and women in Cracow. But that great saving transaction pales in comparison to what happened at Calvary...where the singular, loving gift of a single perfect life...really did make possible the salvation of the entire world. Trust that love. Live in response to that love. And you will be saved.

Excuse my asking, I know it's a very personal question, but...are you saved?

## Romans 12:1-2
### Introductory Comments

The following sermon, "Life on the Altar," explores Romans 12:1-2, the familiar text which opens Paul's section on moral instruction in his epistle. As Dave Bland explains so well, Paul's moral vision for the people of Christ is driven by his theological presuppositions laid out in Romans 1-8, and importantly, must be understood as a community ethic. The momentum of Romans moves toward the question of how the faith community lives. Thus the exhortations in chapters 12-15 are the apex of Paul's correspondence to the church.

The very-visual image of the altar governs this message, locating authentic worship at the place within where we identify our highest value, and pay homage to it by the making of "a living sacrifice," which I understand not as ascetic self-denial (which can be quite narcissistic) but as loving self-donation. Paul's "urging" (*paraklesis*) toward holy living, as both Dave Bland and James Thompson point out, appeals not to my powers of self-control but to the power of God's gospel.

The claim of the text is: every person places his or her life on some altar. Let us respond to the God who has graced us amazingly by offering him our best worship, the very giving of ourselves, that we might undergo not secular conformity but divine transformation.

# Life on the Altar
## Romans 12:1-2

Before Marian Anderson became the 20th century's greatest contralto, she was a young girl who sang in the choir at the Union Baptist Church in Philadelphia. Her church members knew Marian was something special, so they pooled pocket change into "The Fund for Marian Anderson's Future" and sent her to New York City to make her Town Hall debut. But she was not ready, her debut was a critical disaster, and she returned to Philadelphia in disgrace. Marian's depression and embarrassment lasted over a year until—she would say in later years—something her mother told her finally sunk in. "Marian," said her mother, a cleaning woman, "grace must come before greatness. Why don't you think about this failure a little and pray about it a lot?"

Grace must come before greatness. As Romans 12 opens, beginning the section of the letter dealing with Christian behavior, grace comes first. *"Therefore I urge you, brothers, in view of God's mercy..."* For Paul, grace always comes first. The amazing grace of God. Our only hope. But then, he moves directly...not to greatness... but to the altar.

### The conversation

As we investigate Romans 12 this morning, I want you to imagine a conversation. Adelphos and Adelphe, brother and sister, have come from Rome to Corinth, where the apostle Paul is staying. These two young Christians have journeyed all this way because they have some questions about the radical document we call the book of Romans, and they can't wait for Paul to make his promised visit to Rome to have their curiosity satisfied.

> **Paul**:  *So, my young brother and sister in Christ, here we are again. You've come all the way from Rome here to Corinth to interrogate old Paul. May I just say before we resume our conversation, good for you! There is nothing our Lord Jesus wants more of his disciples than intellectual honesty, the inquisitive spirit that asks and seeks and knocks at the door of understanding God's will. Because only as you commit your mind to your God will your mind be renewed, reawakened, reinvigorated…and only then will you be able to test and to approve what God's good, pleasing, and perfect will for us is. Now, where were we?*
>
> **Adelphos**:  Okay, today I want to ask about some things you said in your letter to us…oh, about twelve-sixteenths of the way along. Paul, I have to tell you, I really wish you had used a different word to describe how we're to live our Christian life than the word "*sacrifice.*" What an unpleasant word! When I hear "sacrifice," what I think of are screaming animals being dragged onto stone altars…priests brandishing sharp knives, slitting the throats of innocent little lambs…blood splattered all over everything. Yuck.
>
> **Paul**:  *Well, I'm sorry if I got a little too graphic for you there, but you know what, Adelphos? The lamb on that bloody altar—that's you, my friend! I don't know how to say this in a subtle way: God…wants…you. But what he wants is your life, not your death! The operative word here is "living"…a living sacrifice.*
>
> *Here's what I'm trying to say with the language of sacrifice: Given all that your Abba God has done in extending his amazing grace to you…given that he created*

*you from dirt and breathed his life-breath into you…given that he gave you the right to choose as an autonomous being what you want to do with your life…given that while you were still the sinner you chose to be, he sent Jesus to be your loving brother and your wise teacher and your redeeming Savior and your interceding priest…given that he sent his Holy Spirit to make your life fruitful—given all those mercies and a whole lot more—I appeal to you from the bottom of my heart: Take your life, your everyday, go-to-work, eat-and-sleep, body-and-soul, made-in-the-image-of-God life, and give it back to God. Present it to him as your best worship offering. I know it's not much; it's hardly a "lamb without blemish." But trust me; it's the offering that pleases him most. It's the worship God most wants from you.*

**Adelphe**: But Paul, I thought "worship" was about singing hymns, and praying prayers, and communion and Scripture reading and almsgiving and preaching…and lots of announcements.

*Paul: You're right, Adelphe. The worship of the family of Christ does include all those things. But the vital and indispensable first act of worship is personal consecration, when you present yourself humbly and genuinely before God and say: "Here I am, Lord. Receive me. Forgive me. Mold me. Use me. Send me." More than any song you sing or contribution you give…more than any prayer you may pray, more than all the sermons you may ever preach…your primary act of worship is the giving of YOU.*

*Any single act of the worship of God is meaningless—pointless, a complete waste of your time and God's—if it's not the expression of a LIFE of worship…life that takes God's moral values and social ethics seriously. Here, let me read you something from the Old Book. (Hold on to your hat; this is powerful stuff!)*

*Hear the word of the Lord, you rulers of Sodom;*

*Listen to the law of our God, you people of Gomorrah!*

*"The multitude of your sacrifices—what are they to me?" says the Lord.*

*"I have more than enough of burnt offerings, or rams and the fat of fattened animals;*

*I have no pleasure in the blood of bulls and lambs and goats.*

*When you come to appear before me, who has asked this of you, this trampling of my courts?*

*Stop bringing meaningless offerings! Your incense is detestable to me.*

*New Moons, Sabbaths, and convocations—I cannot bear your evil assemblies.*

*Your New Moon festivals and your appointed feasts my soul hates.*

*They have become a burden to me; I am weary of bearing them.*

*When you spread out your hands in prayer, I will hide my eyes from you; even if you offer many prayers, I will not listen.*

*Your hands are full of blood; wash and make yourselves clean.*

*Take your evil deeds out of my sight!*

*Stop doing wrong, learn to do right!*

*Seek justice, encourage the oppressed.*

*Defend the cause of the fatherless, plead the case of the widow."*

(Isa 1:10-17)

**Adelphos**: Wow, that is strong stuff. So if I'm hearing you, we're defining "worship" not just in terms of what happens between the opening and closing prayers on Sunday…but also by how we treat people between the closing prayer on Sunday and the opening prayer the following Sunday?

**Paul**: *You're hearing me loud and clear. But make no mistake: what we do on Sunday when we come together to worship as the family of Christ is no less important, because it's here that we elevate our hearts—and our standards—by praising God. It's here that we come to our Lord's table and remember that any sacrifice we make pales in comparison to the one he made for us. It's here that we reassert our consecration, our determination not to conform to the pattern of this world.*

**Adelphe**: Oh good, I'm glad you brought that up. What exactly is "the pattern of this world"?

*Paul: Well, that's the problem, Adelphe. The pattern of "this world"—and by "this world" I mean that realm of human activity that functions outside of any concern for the claims of God upon us—that's a pretty unstable pattern, one that's always changing…with every new philosophy out of Athens, every new fashion show from Thebes, every new Caesar in Rome.*

*What I'm saying is that we don't have to be hostages of the culture wars around us…suckers for every new ad campaign: "Buy this kind of chariot. Wear this kind of toga. Drink this kind of wine." We don't have to let this world squeeze us into its latest mold of social acceptability or political correctness. We can resist the pressures to conform with this age. We're big boys and girls! We can say "no" to irresponsible sexual behavior. And mindless materialism. And evil racist and sexist talk. And unconscionable indifference to the poor among us. (Isn't that what Isaiah was talking about?)*

*I'm saying we don't have to stand up and salute every*

*time our confused culture raises its flag. We can resist...
because we have the Holy Spirit of God alive and at work
within us—renewing our minds, clearing our heads—
bringing us back to the one pattern that is changeless...to
the one life matrix that we want our lives to be in
sync with...to the one model of human behavior that is
dependable and rock-solid. What I'm talking about,
Adelphe, is Jesus. His pattern of living and loving is our
constant. As someone has said, "He's the same—yesterday,
today, forever" (Heb 13:8).*

**Adelphe**: I do want to please God with my life, Paul.
But that's the problem with this "living sacrifice"
business—I guess I think I make a pretty shabby offering
on God's altar.

*Paul: You know, I would agree with you, Adelphe, if
all you had to offer God was your own merit, your own
dirty-rag righteousness. In that case, you would make a
pretty sorry offering! But as I told our brothers and sisters
over in Galatia, all of us who were baptized into Christ have
had ourselves clothed with Christ (Gal 3:26). And that
means that we now wear the robes of his righteousness...and
so we are fit for God's altar!*

*Sometimes I think about the marvelous story they tell
about our Lord, how on that Sunday just before the Cross he
rode into Jerusalem on that little donkey, while the crowds
yelled "Hosanna!" at the top of their lungs. (Now Jesus had
obviously made previous arrangements to use that donkey, so
when he sent a couple of the disciples to fetch it, he told them
to say to anyone who asks, "The Master has need of it.") Well,
sometimes I like to think of myself as that little donkey that
Sunday: just doing the job the Master arranged for him to
do. You think that donkey thought all those "Hosannas"
were for him? Nah, I'll bet he was just glad to be someone
the Master needed, glad to be along for the ride.*

*Everybody places their lives on somebody's altar, Adelphe. Your choice of altar is the biggest choice of your life, so choose wisely…because what is most worth dying for…is what is most worth living for.*

### The place of sacrifice

*"Offer your bodies as living sacrifices, holy and pleasing to God—this is your spiritual act of worship"* (Rom 12:2). In every person's life, there is an altar. It's the place where we identify our highest value, our god above all gods, and pay homage…show reverence…worship. We worship what we live for, and we live for what we worship.

And what do you do at an altar? You make a sacrifice. The altar is the place of sacrifice. Everyone recognizes the merit of sacrifice. Ask the great athletes, the great musicians, the great artists, and they'll tell you, they paid a price. ("No pain, no gain.")

But I don't think Paul is saying "sacrifice" here with clinched teeth and a furrowed brow. I think what he has in mind is not only divestment—giving up something—but also investment—giving ourselves *to* something, something wonderful. We hear "sacrifice" and we automatically think "self-denial." But what if we thought more in terms of self-donation…self-contribution… surrendering ourselves to and pouring our best energies into something eternal? Ask the great parents, the great teachers, the great servants of God, and they'll tell you, they do what they do gratuitously…for its own sake…for the love of it.

The greatest act of sacrifice in Scripture, outside the cross, had to be Abraham's willingness to offer Isaac. What a terrible altar-moment that was! But the real issue there, as far as God was concerned, was whether or not

Abraham would trust his covenant son to God. *"You have not withheld FROM ME your son,"* God said (Gen 22:12, emphasis mine, here and below). Abraham trusted Isaac to God. And did you ever notice what Abraham said to the servants just before he and Isaac went up to the place of sacrifice? *"We will worship and then we will come back"* (22:5). Sounds to me like Abraham fully expected to bring Isaac back with him! And when the Lord provided the sacrifice, Abraham had the good sense to call that place *"The Lord Will Provide"* (22:14).

### Living on the altar

*"This is your spiritual act of worship."* You'll never hear a clearer, more personal, more demanding definition of worship than you get right here. We have often spoken of the "five acts of worship" in the early church: prayer, singing, the Lord's Supper, preaching the Word, and giving. (Sometimes we assign greater value to one "act" or another. "Now we come to the Lord's Supper, the most important part of our worship." Or "If the singing isn't really outstanding, I don't feel like I've worshiped.")

But here in Romans 12, Paul identifies the one essential and defining act of worship...and it's not even on the "five acts" list! *"Offer God yourself,"* he says, *"This is your spiritual [reasonable; rightly-understood] worship of God."* Grace first, Paul says, grace always comes first...then comes worship, then the altar...and the sacrifice is you. That's right, climb right up on the altar. NO, it won't kill you. Just the opposite: it will infuse you and invigorate you with LIFE as you have never known before!

Life in Christ—Paul says—is "life on the altar." And that's a lifestyle that calls us both to investment and divestment…no small challenge. I recall a popular Christian poster from the '60s which said, "The problem with living sacrifices is that they keep crawling off the altar." We worship what we live for, and we live for what we worship. And that's why—Paul says—we must not, dare not allow the values of this secular world to be the mold to which we conform our hearts and minds. *"The pattern of this world"* cannot become the model by which our families and vocations and dreams are measured and shaped.

But cultural pressure to conform is so strong. And so effective. I heard a man who had been to the Far East explain how they sometimes train monkeys to salute, to entertain the tourists. (I warn you, this is unpleasant.) The "trainer" puts the monkey in a room with a dog. Once a day the trainer walks in, goes straight to the dog, and orders, "Salute!" Of course the dog doesn't salute; dogs can't salute. Then the trainer beats the dog, while the monkey watches. After several days of this, the trainer walks in, commands the dog to "Salute!" and when the poor dog doesn't, he kills the dog. He then turns to the monkey and commands, "Salute!" And the monkey almost always salutes. We learn the lesson early on: there's a price to be paid for going against the mainstream of popular culture. Walking the high road of kingdom values may call for sacrifice—actual forfeiture—of rights, or status, or profitability. (Omni Hotels found that out recently; they made the decision not to provide adult films in their rooms, and it cost them an estimated $1.8 million a year.)

It certainly will call for creative thinking and living. In Lee Hardy's book *The Fabric of This World*, he tells of an old and distinguished law firm in Grand Rapids,

Michigan, which changed the way their firm did business. The partners in the firm, active churchmen, decided to limit the firm's claims upon their employees' lives. Lawyers were held accountable for fewer billable hours than the average law firm. Hourly workers were seldom asked to work long overtime hours. All employees were given more vacation time and encouraged "to recognize the importance of...their family, community, religious, and other like commitments unrelated to the practice of law." Salaries were slightly lower (due to fewer work hours), but their people were sharper, fresher, happier... at no loss of competitive edge in the legal community. (Come to think of it, it's hard to say where the "sacrifice" is in this illustration.)

Let me put my cards on the table. Every Sunday I'm up here to try to convince you (and myself) to take God more seriously. Put another way, my modest aim every Sunday is nothing less than to *convert* you. And believe you me, I'm not the only one trying to convert you. So is Hollywood and NBC and Fox and the *LA Times* and *Newsweek* and *GQ* and *Cosmopolitan* and the Republican Party and the Democratic Party and the NRA and Greenpeace and Coca-Cola and Toyota and Calvin Klein and Ralph Lauren....

The competition—for our attention, for our dollar, for our children, for our very souls—is stiff. The stakes couldn't be higher. That's why we must be so very cautious, so very intentional, about whom we "salute"... about whose altar we choose.

### Conformed to his likeness

A recent exhibit on our campus featured "The Thinker," the bronze figure of a man deep in thought which may be the most recognizable sculpture in the Western world. It was cast from a mold by the French artist Auguste Rodin. How did he do it? First, the master artist created the original masterpiece. That became the model from which a mold was made, and from the mold, reproductions of the original were cast.

The Master Artist is the Creator. His master work is Christ, the measure of life as the Giver of life intended. And here's the grace (where everything begins): from before the beginning of time it was in the mind of the Creator that we be *"conformed to the likeness of his Son"* (Rom 8:29). The Son is the God-created mold into which we may pour our hearts and minds and values and dreams. How incredible! How audacious! That we might hope to be little reproductions of Jesus! Maybe that's why Max Lucado says we sing *"Amazing Grace,"* and not *"Amazing Logic."*

And we…are being transformed into his likeness with ever-increasing glory, which comes from the Lord, who is the Spirit" (2 Cor 3:18).

## *Romans 12:3-21*
## *Introductory Comments*

What does it mean to be a church member? This text offers an opportunity to take a fresh look at some familiar church concepts, such as the rich analogical possibilities (see Stephen Farris) of "the body of Christ," the much-misunderstood concept of "membership," and the challenge of "brotherly love."

This sermon, building on Paul's "living sacrifice" paradigm of Romans 12:1-2, focuses on Christian lifestyle. 12:9-21 is a list of moral imperatives in need of proper context, lest it be reduced to a collection of individualistic moralisms; ours is primarily a community ethic, an expression of our identity as "one body."

In addressing the formidable task of being a church of Jesus Christ, it is important that the sermon give voice to those negative experiences that naturally result from the humanity and the diversity of the local church. The message, like the text which defines it, strives to keep the companion objectives of unity and diversity in redemptive tension, appealing both to the prayerful intent of Jesus (John 17) and the original plea of the American Restoration Movement.

The claim of the text on the hearer, then, is this: Given that we "belong" to one another in Christ, we find concrete ways to love one another, nurture our unity (embracing all members of the Body), and model the love of Christ to the watching world.

## *Corpus Christi*
## *Romans 12:3-21*

Did you hear what Paul said? He said we belong to one another. So how do you feel about that? Doesn't that rankle your rugged individualism? Stifle your independent spirit? Go against the grain of your First Amendment rights to do whatever you please and if the other guy has a problem with that well then that's just too bad?

The fact is, it's hard "belonging" to one another like we do in the church of Jesus Christ. For one thing, the church is made up of real people...and real people have an annoyingly-high incidence rate of messing up.

With the start of baseball season this week, I'm thinking about our Dodgers and remembering a time they played in Brooklyn, and were pretty lousy. They say a Dodger fan was listening to the game on his radio, when a friend passed by. "Hey!" he said, "the Dodgers have three men on base!" "Yeah?" said the friend, who obviously knew the Dodgers well, "Which base?"

The church is like that. We mess up, stumble around, make all kinds of goofs running the bases. The church, like the world around it, is a pretty grace-needy bunch.

### Corpus Christi?

But remarkably, Paul here in Romans 12—and throughout his epistles—looks at the likes of us and pronounces us *"the body of Christ."* Just what does that mean?

Have you ever been in a cadaver lab at a medical school? I have, and it's a singularly disconcerting experience. Picture a large, well-lit room, smelling of strong chemicals, and on tables all around it…are bodies. Once, you can't help but think, this was a person: he played, pondered, laughed, dreamed. But now there's just a "body"—a "corpse" (from the Latin for body). Without God's breath of life, the person that once was there, is no longer there.

Is that what we mean when we call the church the *corpus Christi*, "the body of Christ"? I must say, I've known some pretty cadaverous churches. All vital signs say, "No life here; the breath of God is nowhere to be found." The coroner's report reads as it did in Sardis (Rev 3:1): *"Dead."*

Is that what Jesus has in mind when he says, *"I will build my church"* (Matt 16:18)? Is that what Paul means here by *"the body of Christ"*? How can I say this strongly enough? NO! The biblical image of what Christ intends for his community could not be more diametrically opposite. The church that allows itself to be built by Jesus is going to be—like Jesus—vibrant, active, brave, fruitful…alive!

### The conversation

Now I need you to imagine that when the church in Rome reads this epistle from Paul in their assembly, two fairly-new Christians—we'll call them Adelphe and Adelphos—are listening. They are so intrigued by this message that they trace Paul down in the city of Corinth to ask him a few questions. By listening in, maybe we can enter into the God-breathed conversation that is the letter to the Romans.

**Adelphe**: Paul, you've been pretty patient with my brother Adelphos and me, answering our questions about your letter to our fellowship in Rome. But I suppose by now it's obvious to you that we're not here just to talk ideas and doctrines with you. We're having some real *problems* at church back home: arguments, controversies, factions. Some folks say they don't see the point of assemblies; they say they can worship God more effectively in private. Others want to break off and form fellowship groups that are more heterogeneous and comfortable with each other. And some say we've got too many slaves in the church...that members like that discredit the church in the eyes of the community. What do you say to all that?

*Paul: Okay Adelphe, let's get real basic. Peter and some of the other veteran leaders told me about a day in Galilee, near Caesarea Philippi, when Jesus told them, "I'm going to build a church, a fellowship of men and women, that will shake the very gates of Hades with their courage and their joy and their kindness and their love"* (Matt 16:18). *He had in mind a church that would be like no human enterprise ever known. A church that would be his body on this earth after his return to heaven.*

*Well, that church he was talking about is now a reality! Jesus built his church. He* continues *to build his church... and you and Adelphos and I are it...at least, parts of it. Like members of a human body, you're members of his body today. And if you don't act like dismembered members, your lives can be extensions of his life on the earth here and now.*

*You see, this is a radical new way of thinking about inter-personal relationships. If you grew up Jewish, you thought of yourselves as connected to one another by your clan, your ethnicity; you were an extension of the holy family of Israel. If you grew up Roman—blessed to be a citizen of Rome as I am—you thought of yourself as connected to* *one another by your political status; you were an extension of the mighty Empire. But get this: if you are making "the living sacrifice"—voluntarily placing your life on the altar of Christ for him to receive and forgive and use as a blessing to the world—*then *you can legitimately think of yourself as members of one single body, of one vital, vibrant life-force: the body of Jesus Christ. We're attached to everybody else in this Jesus-organism that is his church.*

**Adelphos**: When you say "everybody," do you mean...everybody?

*Paul: Everybody! The Jews and the Gentiles. The slaves and the free. Males and females. The eggheads and the anti-intellectuals. The libs and the fundies. The rednecks and the snobs. The nerds and the super-cool. The nuts and the flakes. The babies and the geezers (like me). Everybody! One body.*

**Adelphos**: So, when you wrote us that "Each member *belongs* to all the others," you really *meant* that? You weren't just using apostolic literary license?

*Paul: You're right, I meant it! God has joined us to each other. We are attached...connected...linked... merged...mixed...combined...unified by God. (That's why we need to* act *unified.) Say, I've been toying with a Latin phrase that I think captures what Christ intended for his church: "e pluribus unum." What do you think?*

**Adelphos**: Let's see, I should know this. "From many...one." Very nice, Paul. Very catchy. But my question about all this is...Why? *Why* has God joined us to one another? It's *hard* being joined! It's often a lot easier being independent and free of others. Is this God's way of amusing himself, watching us try to put up with each other? Or is this just his way of testing how committed we are?

*Paul: I'll admit we do test one another's patience in this Body of ours. But what it comes down to is this: we are attached to one another because we need each other. We need each other for spiritual strength and survival; maybe you've noticed—it's a cold, tough, lonely world out there. We need each other for optimum productivity; we can do so much more working together (a chopped-off finger—pardon my analogy—can't accomplish much, can it?). We need each other because a burden shared is a burden greatly diminished...and a joy shared is a joy multiplied!*

**Adelphe**: Okay, I'll grant you, Paul...when it works, it works better than anything in this world. But sometimes the church doesn't live up to its calling, and that's when it's hard being connected to other Christians. They can be such a pain sometimes...so...

*Paul: Stubborn? Short-sighted? Petty?*

**Adelphe**: Yeah! And insensitive, and inconsiderate, and hypocritical....

*Paul: And proud. And legalistic. And prejudiced. And stingy. And cowardly. And unreliable. And inconsistent. And worldly. And weak. And sinful. Don't get me started, Adelphe! (I guess you already have, haven't you?)*

*Look, I know the church is full of sinners. We're a grace-needy bunch if there ever was one! If you're looking for a perfect church to be connected to, by all means, become a member of it...but you need to know this: the moment you join it, it will cease to be a perfect church!*

*Being connected to a family of diverse, fallible, grace-needy human beings takes all the patience and determination and prayer we can muster some days. In point of fact, it takes nothing less than the Spirit of God— I'm talking supernatural assistance here—to keep the church unified. It takes all the charismata—the spiritual* gifts—with which God has blessed us, to keep the body of Christ working together as one body.

As we live out our oneness, there are some commitments to one another, some decisions to love and cooperate, that we have to maintain every day. I included a list of some of them in my letter to your congregations in Rome. I call my list "Twenty-One Ways to Love Your Neighbor" (not "Leave Your Lover"…"Love your Neighbor"):

[If you'd like to follow along in your Bibles, this is based on Romans 12:9-21, with a lot of help from Eugene Peterson.]

1—Love your brother and sister in Christ from your heart; don't fake it.

2—Run for dear life from evil; hold on for dear life to good.

3—Be a true friend—faithful, devoted, affectionate.

4—Be generous in honoring one another; don't worry about any credit due you (God will take care of that).

5—Keep the flame of the Spirit kindled; don't let yourself get burned out (you're not much use to the Lord if you let that happen).

6—Be a hopeful person; cheerfully expect God to work in all things for his good and yours.

7—Don't quit when hard times come (and they will).

8—Pray. Pray constantly. Pray honestly. Pray earnestly. Pray expectantly. Pray!

9—Help needy Christians every way you can; God's gifts are yours to share, not to hoard.

10—Be creative in your hospitality; look for new ways to make others feel accepted and valued and loved.

*11—Bless your adversaries and your detractors (no cursing under your breath allowed).*

*12—Celebrate the joys, achievements, and victories of others, and share the tears, disappointments, and defeats of others. (Remember: a burden shared is a burden diminished, and a joy shared is a joy multiplied.)*

*13—Get along with one another; there's no such thing as "irreconcilable differences" in the body of Christ.*

*14—Don't be stuck up. (Don't ever forget: God made you from dirt.)*

*15—Be friendly with people who may at first seem unimpressive to you. (Don't ever forget: God made them in his image.)*

*16—Don't hit back; somebody has to break the deadly cycle of retribution and retaliation.*

*17—In all your dealings public and private, make it your goal to be a man or woman of honor and integrity.*

*18—It's not always possible, but when it is, live at peace with everyone whose life touches yours.*

*19—You are not the final judge and jury of humankind—God is; so why not leave the ultimate judgment and justice to him?*

*20—Surprise your antagonists with unexpected generosity and kindness (it will blow their minds, I guarantee you!).*

*21—Don't let evil get the best of you; get the best of evil by doing good.*

**Adelphos**: Well, we've obviously got a lot of work to do back home at church in Rome. And from what I've heard about church life here in Corinth, this extension of the body of Christ has got a long way to go, too.

*Paul: Well, we've all got a long way to go, don't we, Adelphos? Each and every one of us. But we can't let discouragement knock us off course, can't let human failure make us cynical or pessimistic. And we can't lower the high standard Jesus set for us. The stakes are just too high.*

*We—the church of Jesus Christ—his fickle, fallible church—we're the best look many people are going to get at Christ! The best shot they'll have at really being loved. The best chance they'll have to be part of one fellowship in this crazy, selfish, individualized world where the criteria for acceptance is not whiter teeth and fresher breath…where weakness is not considered a liability but a shared struggle …where failure and pain are not grist for the gossip mill but burdens to be borne together…where vulnerability can be risked, and doubt and frustration expressed, and sins confessed and overcome. The one society that will last forever.*

### A unified, diverse body

"Body" is Paul's favorite image for the Church (Rom 12:5; 1 Cor 12:27; Eph 4:12; Col 1:18). It's a brilliant and dynamic metaphor that captures two absolutely essential qualities of Christ's Church: our unity…and our diversity.

In his final hours, Jesus was praying for the unity of his disciples: *"that they may be one"* (John 17:11). No doubt the church's founder knew what a challenge that would be for us: Jews and Gentiles, slaves and free, males and females, nuts and flakes, and all the rest. That's why Paul talks about the gifts of the Spirit here in Romans 12. Only the Holy Spirit of God could bring unity out of such diversity!

And where the Spirit is, there is LIFE. That's why I wish I could get my hands on the guy that first used the word "member" to refer to a name on a mailing list. Steal my wallet, and you'll discover that I'm a "member" of AAA of Southern California, the Blockbuster Video Club, American Airlines Frequent Flyer Club, and Ogden's One-Hour Cleaners VIP Club (20% off all shirts), to name but a few. "Membership" in those groups gets me a discount. Being a "member" of the Body of Christ—being organically and redemptively connected to the King of Glory—brings me LIFE!

When I first arrived to preach in Falls Church, Virginia, I had to be initiated into the local phenomenon known as the Ladies' Bible Class Soup Day. On the appointed Soup Day, each sister who came to LBC brought a pot of soup, any kind of soup—vegetable, chicken, tomato, bean—any kind. And when they got there (get this), they poured all their soups into one big pot! What could I do when I was invited to join them for lunch? You can't say no to the Ladies Bible Class. So, I braced myself and dug into this brown, nondescript-looking gruel and it was pretty tasty! I enjoyed many more Soup Days after that. Every time the soup de jour was a little different (though always brown), but invariably good, and quite nourishing. Don't ask me to explain it; I just accepted it as a gift of God, and a parable of *koinonia*.

In the human body—Paul points out—it is our diversity of form and function that makes us so wonderfully versatile, so very handy. That's why we can walk and talk and digest and laugh and write and jump and throw and hug and kiss and dream.

And, that's why in the body of Christ—he goes on—

we can serve and teach and encourage and contribute and lead and (here's a big one) show mercy.

But, have you noticed, in most human societies—churches included—diversity is often seen, not as a blessing but a curse, not as a godsend but a threat. So unconsciously (maybe even consciously), we find ourselves avoiding it, disparaging it, discouraging it. It sure sounds like the fellowship in Rome had diversity issues: *looking down on*, and *judging*, and even potentially *destroying* one another over disputable matters (Rom 14:1,9-10,13,15;15:7).

Nobody said diversity was easy. It may not even be pretty—like brown soup. But it's really tasty, and so good for you. And the fact is, I believe, God delights in our diversity. In the church Jesus wishes to be building, diversity is not something merely to be tolerated, but something to be encouraged and cherished…as evidence of God's hand in shaping the body according to his heterogeneous design: *"But in fact God has arranged the parts in the body, every one of them, just as he wanted them to be"* (1 Cor 12:18).

### A unity movement

The movement that gave rise to the Churches of Christ in this country—the American Restoration Movement—was, let us never forget, a *unity* movement. Alexander Campbell in his essay on "Christian Union" said "Union and truth combined are omnipotent."

On the same night that Jesus prayed that his disciples be *"one,"* he also prayed that they might be *"sanctified by the truth"* (John 17:17).

Unity and truth. That's a tough balance and a difficult alliance to maintain. Pursue *only* truth, and you can end up with a rigid, close-minded exclusivism. Pursue *only* unity, and you can end up with an easy and flabby ecumenism. As a brotherhood, can we afford to forsake either goal in exclusive pursuit of the other, when our Lord prayed that his Church be known for both? I believe our brother Paul would say, "God forbid!"

We can't afford to act like a divided (dismembered!) body, because Paul says, *"Each member belongs to all the others"* (Rom 12:5). That must mean that we each belong to *all* our brothers and sisters...not just to those who live in our zip code or sit in our quadrant of the church building...or belong to the Churches of Christ. We *"belong to,"* are connected by Christ to, *all* who make up the family of God.

### A different society

You see, this society of Jesus is different, different from all other societies on this earth. We've got at least twenty-one ways to love people here. We accept one another here. We honor one another. We weep with those who weep here, and rejoice with those who rejoice here. We are accountable to one another here. We have very high expectations for one another here. And we extend great mercy towards one another here...because we're a grace-needy bunch, and we *belong* to one another here.

We're members of the body of Christ. And when the church is being the church, being the physical presence of Christ in this world, there is nothing on this earth more extraordinary.

I heard Terry Johnson tell about a visit he made to a Church of Christ in the Oklahoma City area. He preached that Sunday, he said, and then stayed around for the business meeting after worship. Sounds like it was a fairly typical business meeting. The Education Committee reported they were able to send $1000 to support a training workshop. The Benevolence Committee reported that they'd collected a large supply of canned goods to send to the children's home. The Missions Committee reported that a former member, Jesus Castro, was now in Columbia preaching the gospel there.

Fine, fine. But what's so unusual about a church doing all that? Here it is: this particular congregation meets in the El Reno Federal Reformatory...and all its members are prisoners.

The Education Committee sent $1000 for a prison ministry workshop. The Benevolence Committee collected canned goods, from the prison commissary, for the children's home. And Jesus Castro, the missionary, was a released prisoner who had returned to his native Columbia and was now baptizing people into Christ, just as he had been in the El Reno Federal Reformatory.

Now...could I interest any of you in a most unusual bowl of soup?

## Romans 13
## Introductory Comments

This sermon was preached on Easter Sunday, although Romans 13 is not specifically about resurrection. Faced with the choice of either stepping outside Romans (and the sermon series) for a more resurrection-specific text or sticking with the next text Romans gave me, I chose the latter. I wanted our holiday worshippers to get a taste of our conversation with Paul's epistle. And, I thought this text offered an excellent example of the challenge and glory of resurrection-shaped living.

In Romans 13 we have a further application of the community ethic that for Paul, as Dave Bland explains, is undergirded and shaped by Scripture and the cross. I used the dialogue between Paul and my two imaginary young people to work with some of the ethical themes—submitting to authorities, loving your neighbor—in the text, while reminding listeners of the centrality of Scripture. The final move in the sermon was back to the resurrection event, when the "death-defying" power of God broke into our space and time and revolutionized our moral imaginations.

The claim of this text: Because we are part of the community of those clothed with the resurrected Christ, *"let us put aside the deeds of darkness and put on the armor of light"* (13:12), i.e., live as exemplary citizens and loving neighbors.

## Death Defiance
## Romans 13

It is one of the best-known stories from ancient church history. In the summer of 386 AD, a young professor of rhetoric sat in the garden of his friend Alypias, weeping because he was so unhappy with his immoral way of life. He heard children playing nearby, and they were singing a little song which sounded like, "*Tolle lege...Take up and read.*" He saw a scroll nearby, a scroll of Paul's letter to the Romans, and he "took it up" and read: *"The night is nearly over; the day is almost here. So let us put aside the deeds of darkness and put on the armor of light"* (Rom 13:12). The young man would later write, "At the end of this sentence, a clear light flooded my heart." Augustine had found a new way to live...a death-defying way to live.

The Easter tradition—named after the Norse goddess Eastre, who was honored by a festival centuries before Christ—has gotten, like most religious holidays, pretty cluttered. It's become a day overflowing with eggs and chocolates and lilies and bonnets and bunnies and crosses and life and death. Let's cut through the clutter by proclaiming what *every* Sunday—Lord's Day—Resurrection Day—proclaims: that there is in Christ a life that is stronger than death. So now let us all sing *"Joy to the World."*

### Death-defying life

When I was a little guy—like a lot of little guys—I loved to go to the circus. There was this particular expression I always associated with the circus, one they always used to describe acts like the high-wire performers. The expression was "death-defying." "Ladies and gentlemen, boys and girls, children of all ages, if you will direct your attention high above the center ring, the Flying Zambonis will now risk their lives in a death-defying display...." Death-defying...wow!

There's something pretty exciting, pretty entertaining about high-wire walkers and lion tamers and stock car drivers and Russian roulette players and other death-defiers. But the story we tell at Easter—and every time we come to the Lord's Table—is something very different. It's about a way of living that defies death... not by seeing how close we can get to the precipice of it without tumbling in...but by living *life* to the fullest, by living out values and staking our lives on realities that are stronger than death itself, by living with joy and grace and fearlessness, by discovering, as Augustine did, a better way of living: *"putting aside the deeds of darkness...clothing ourselves with the Lord Jesus Christ"* (Rom 13:12,14).

Nobody ever explained it to me, but I'm guessing that the beloved tradition of the Easter-egg hunt has something to do with the search for *life*. An egg is after all a little genesis-package, a life container. (So why do we boil the life right out of it, or switch to plastic and stuff it with treats?) Today we're going in search of life—revolutionary, death-defying life—and we're going to look for it in Romans 13.

### The conversation

To try to get at Paul's notion of a death-defying worldview, let's first imagine a first-century conversation that Paul might have had with some young Christians who heard the book of Romans read in their assembly, and decided to seek out the apostle for a bit of cross-examination.

**Adelphos**: Okay Paul, Adelphe and I have discussed this, and the subject for our little discussion today is *politics*. The last time we talked, we discussed the matter of your exasperating devotion to your own people, the Jews. Despite how many of them have treated you and rejected your message, you keep going back to preach in the synagogues, and you hold out hope for the salvation of Israel.

But now let's talk about your equally-annoying loyalty to Rome and its government. Allow me to quote directly from your epistle to us: *"Everyone must submit himself to the governing authorities, for there is no authority except that which God has established. The authorities that exist have been established by God"* (13:1). Come on, Paul, give me a break! Submit to Rome? Do you actually expect us to accept the totalitarian rule of Caesar as something from *God*?

**Paul:** *Adelphos, there are a couple of issues here: credibility and citizenship. First, we believers are always called to walk the high road of decency and integrity. Christians, above all people, should be law-abiding. (There's no place where that's more important than in Rome, where our fellowship is under a cloud of constant suspicion.) Why should people out there in the world at large listen to anything we have to say about Jesus if we aren't being good neighbors and responsible citizens?*

*As good citizens, we should be doing all we can to show proper respect for the governing authorities over us. We owe conditional loyalty to the state: not absolute loyalty—that belongs to our Lord Christ alone—but conditional loyalty. The social order is not likely to change any day soon, and we must do all we can to live peaceably and productively within it. Christ has called us to a revolutionary way of living…but we are not anarchists.*

*The pax Romana—the Roman peace, the current absence of warfare—allows people like you and me to travel about freely and in relative safety throughout the Empire. It allows us to spread the good news of God's love and grace all over the Mediterranean world and beyond. That political circumstance serves the purposes of God. We should be thankful for that.*

**Adelphos**: But what do you mean when you say, *"The authorities have been established by God"?*

*Paul: Okay, let's begin here: God is the ultimate Authority. Not Nero. Not the Roman Senate. The human government we're currently under is obviously an authoritarian one, claiming an absolute authority over us, and wielding it at times in a cruel and godless way. There's little or no respect for the one God in the house of Caesar or in the halls of the Senate.*

*But the concept of government, the principle of a local or national ruling authority…that is God-ordained. There must be a governing structure over any community if there is to be order and safety, and fairness and justice. When the powers-that-be are functioning the way God intends—keeping the peace, rewarding good people, punishing criminal people—then they are functioning as servants of God (whether they intend to or not). That's why we need governors, policemen, soldiers, tax collectors, judges…lawyers.*

**Adelphe**: Lawyers?

*Paul: Yes, lawyers.*

**Adelphe**: Okay, but what about when the governing authorities make unrighteous demands of us?

*Paul: That's why I said we owe "conditional loyalty" to the state. If the state calls us to disobey a clear command from our God, then we say "No" to the state. If Caesar calls us to address him as our divine Lord, then we say "No" to*

*Caesar. If it comes down to an obvious choice between the standards of God and the laws of Rome, then we break the laws of Rome: civil disobedience.*

*In the meantime, we say "Yes" to all of the demands of the state that we can. Remember what our Lord taught us: "Give Caesar what is Caesar's, and God what is God's"* (Matt 22:21). *As our brother Peter says, "Let us live such good lives among the pagans that they might see God in us and glorify Him"* (1 Peter 2:12). *So, for Pete's sake, and God's, let's be the best Christian neighbors and citizens we can be! That means we will teach our children to respect those who have authority over us. And we will honor our governing officials every way we in good conscience can. And…will pay our taxes.*

**Adelphe**:   Pay our taxes? I was afraid you were serious about that! Don't you know what today is? It's April 15th!

**Paul**:   *I know, I know. Look, nobody enjoys paying taxes. We may not like the amount of taxes the government collects, but surely we recognize that the principle of taxation is a valid one: sharing in the costs of the greater community.*

*But let's not lose our perspective here, children. How much control can Rome exert over our lives? She can tax our income. She can post her soldiers in our cities. She can strut, and decree, and flex her military muscle any way she chooses. She can even—and may well soon—imprison our spokesmen (like yours truly) and try to silence our gospel. But she will never claim our highest loyalty! She will never capture our hearts! She will never have our souls!*

**Adelphe**:   Speaking of taxes, you did talk in your letter about indebtedness. You say, *"Let no debt remain outstanding except the continuing debt to love one another."* What exactly is this *"continuing debt of love"*?

**Paul**: *Well, I always think first of the cross. Where Jesus paid the debt for our sinfulness: paid the debt he did not owe, the debt we could not pay. We may pay the government what we owe (and then some). But we can never pay back God for his grace and forgiveness, not to mention his good world and all the gifts of life and nature and family. So how do we at least attempt to respond adequately to God's love, try to in some sense "pay it back"? By loving each other.*

*Remember something else Jesus said: Love God, love your neighbor: that's the whole Law wrapped up in one concise package (Matt 22:37-40). Love has always been what the commands of God are about. Take the Ten Commandments. Ever notice how all those negatives, those prohibitives, become affirmatives, when you translate them into the love ethic?*

*"You shall not commit adultery" becomes "You shall love your wife or husband—totally, fully, exclusively."*

*"You shall not murder" turns into "You shall determine to love your fellow man—actively, patiently, constructively."*

*"You shall not steal" translates to "You shall be a giver, a helper, a benefactor to others."*

*And "You shall not covet" gets restated like this: "You shall know the peace of God that makes you grateful, gracious, and content."*

*This is our revolutionary way of living! This is how we walk the high road of decency and integrity. This is how we live as good neighbors and citizens. And when we do, the light of Christ will begin to penetrate—and dissipate—the darkness around us. Now is the time, my children, for Christians to wake up and act like people who have been resurrected: delivered from the darkness to walk in the light.*

*Time is precious! We can't afford to fritter away these priceless daylight hours with silly self-indulgence, or*

*dangerous sexual dalliances, or childish bickering and jeal-*
*ousies. Instead of lazing around in raggedy old lifestyles, we*
*need to wake up, clean up, and dress up: put on the very best*
*outfits we've got—our Jesus-clothes (we were clothed with his*
*very nature when we were baptized, remember?)—and get*
*busy living resurrection lives!*

### In the garden

This is something I wrote a few Easters ago; it's
entitled, *"In the Garden,"* and it's based on John 20.

*It is so quiet*
  *here outside the city walls,*
  *here away from the pilgrim masses,*
  *here in this place of the dead.*
*Now...where is it?*
  *It was so much easier to find*
    *in broad daylight*
    *with the soldiers keeping watch.*
  *Yes, here it is, this is the one:*
    *the borrowed resting place,*
    *the parting gift of a secret friend.*
*But something's not right here.*
  *A trick of the shadows? No.*
  *No, the stone really has been shoved aside*
    *and the grave really is...empty.*
*Spread the news! Peter! John! Everyone!*
  *And the men come*
    *and the men look,*
    *and the men leave,*
  *shaking their heads*
    *in bewilderment*
    *and belief.*
*Now it is quiet again,*

*and now the tears come,*
> *born of grief and confusion and love.*
*But who are these new watchmen,*
> *luminous and otherworldly,*
> *now keeping vigil*
> *over an empty grave?*
*In the faint light, a silhouette stirs:*
*familiar somehow,*
*but a gardener, surely.*
> *"Whom do you seek...so tearfully?"*
> *"I seek the body of my Lord."*
*In answer, a single word.*
> *A name. Your name.*
> *"Mary."*
*Then Mary knew.*
*And from that moment in the garden*
*we too have known,*
*we sons of Adam and daughters of Eve,*
*that neither life nor death*
*would ever again be the same.*

Why did she come? Why so early? Why alone? Was it unfinished business? (For "closure," we would say today.) Whatever Mary's reasons, she didn't come for a front-row seat at a resurrection. Jesus was dead. (She was there at the cross, right next to Mary. She heard him: "It's finished," he said.) Jesus was dead, and that was that, and she was just going to have to deal with it and get on with her life.

So Mary brings her grief here to this place of the dead...her worst fears...her broken dreams...to bury them. And instead, in this place of grief and broken dreams, she finds...Jesus...alive, again, never to die again!

### Death-defying power

> And if Christ has not been raised, our preaching
> is useless and so is your faith. More than that, we
> are then found to be false witnesses about God,
> for we have testified about God that he raised
> Christ from the dead. But he did not raise him if
> in fact the dead are not raised. For if the dead are
> not raised, then Christ has not been raised either.
> And if Christ has not been raised, your faith is
> futile; you are still in your sins. Then those also
> who have fallen asleep in Christ are lost. If only
> for this life we have hope in Christ, we are to be
> pitied more than all men. But Christ has indeed
> been raised from the dead.... (1 Cor 15:14-20)

We Christians—Paul told the Corinthians—are folks
who put all our eggs in one basket: Resurrection. It was
the ultimate death-defying act. And not merely one
amazing moment in time. This was a force that has now
been set loose in this world:

> And if the Spirit of him who raised Jesus from the
> dead is living in you, he who raised Christ from
> the dead will also give life to your moral bodies
> through the Spirit, who lives in you. (Rom 8:11)

The power that resurrected Jesus that Sunday...is a
death-defying power. Jesus the resurrected one says:

> I defy the death of your hopes for
> forgiveness, and reconciliation, and joy.
> I defy the power of your sin to make you live
> in guilt and shame and regret.

I defy the power of your fear to make you timid and cowardly and faint-hearted.

I defy the power of your own death to end your life and separate you from God.

## Romans 14-15
## Introductory Comments

This sermon from Romans 14-15 was preached on the last Sunday of the university's spring term in a service which included the recognizing of graduating seniors. Agreeing with Mark Love that Romans is a "pastoral document" that "reaches its pastoral conclusion in 15:7" ("*Welcome one another*"), I wanted to utilize the pastoral themes and directives in this section to exhort the seniors—and everyone else—to "find themselves" within a community of faith. Becoming who God intended us to be is meant to happen in the faith-provoking, Word-nurtured, grace-rich environment of a church of Jesus Christ. This I believe was the claim of this text for this occasion.

A word about my fictional conversations in these sermons. "The epistles," James Thompson writes, "are a portion of the conversation between Paul and his listeners." My imagined dialogue in each sermon attempts to capture that conversational quality of Romans. The use of contemporary, Americanized language may sound dissonant in some ears, and so there is admittedly some risk here. But Romans is a gospel message that was—again citing Thompson—"not an exercise in academic theology, but...[Paul's] response to a crisis, both in his own life and in the churches." The possibility of today's listener being caught up in a fresh, personal conversation with God's living Word is surely worth some carefully-considered homiletical risk.

## Now I Become Myself
## Romans 14-15

On this Senior Sunday when we honor our graduating seniors, I begin with an ominous word of warning about the Real World you're about to enter: Watch out! It's a perilous place!

But then, no less so than the world you're leaving. Why, just this past week (the day after April Fool's Day, to be precise) here on campus, a brand-new copy machine appeared in Appleby Center. And someone— don't ask me who, because I know who—placed a sign above the new machine which read, "This new copier is voice-activated. Be sure to speak loudly and distinctly into the machine." And for the rest of the day, I understand, you could overhear gullible faculty members in the copy room saying, loudly and distinctly, things like, "Thirty copies. Collate. No staple. Activate...now...please?" Oh yes, this world is a perilous place.

### Your primary task

A friend of mine who used to teach at a large California university tells of an encounter with a senior physics major, who came by his office at about this point in his last semester. "I'm graduating with a good degree," he said, "but after four years here, I'm leaving without having found answers to most of the main questions I came here with, questions such as: Who am I? What is life about? What should *my* life be about?"

Those really are the main questions, aren't they? Can any education that doesn't equip us to answer the main questions really claim to be "higher" education? In today's bulletin, you'll find a piece of verse by May Sarton

( *"Now I Become Myself"*):
> *Now I become myself.*
> *It's taken time, many years and places.*
> *I have been dissolved and shaken,*
> *Worn other people's faces….*

Someone has said that life is "one prolonged identity crisis." And Parker Palmer contends that our lives are ongoing "experiments with truth." But all that sounds pretty precarious, doesn't it? Experiments are so trial-and-error, so experimental! But is there a more primary spiritual task than this, the quest for my true self?

True, there are some inherent dangers in the "Who am I?" business: it can turn into a narcissistic, self-absorbed expedition. But I believe the biblical concept of "calling," or "vocation" (from the Latin word for "voice") legitimizes and focuses the question. What has GOD called me to do with my life? How can the gifts GOD has given me be best put to use in my life?

If "I gotta be me"—and I believe God says, "You gotta! You think I created you to be somebody else?"—then how can I be the *authentic* me...or else I'll spend my life *"wearing other people's faces"*? Old Rabbi Zusya, they say, used to tell his students, "In the coming world, God will not ask me, 'Why were you not Abraham, or why were you not Moses?' But he may ask me, 'Why were you not Zusya?'"

**Accept one another in the process.**

Today our study of the book of Romans brings us to chapters 14 and 15. As Paul brings his magnificent letter near its close, we're going to hear him talking a lot about—not so much the process of self-discovery—but how we deal with one another in the body of Christ in the midst of that process. Listen as I read some key verses, and see if you can catch the common, recurring theme:

> *Accept him whose faith is weak.* (14:1)
> *Who are you to judge?* (14:4)
> *Why do you judge your brother?* (14:10)
> *Let us stop passing judgment on one another.* (14:13)
> *Do not destroy your brother.* (14:15)
> *Make every effort to do what leads to peace.* (14:19)
> *We ought to bear with the failings of the weak.* (15:1)
> *May God give you a spirit of unity.* (15:5)
> *Accept one another, just as Christ accepted you.* (15:7)

Paul's directive is pretty clear, isn't it? While we are in the midst of this uneven, rigorous, essential process of "becoming ourselves"—and when are we not?—we're going to need to extend a lot of grace to one another! The church is a fellowship of men and women "in process"...that spiritual process is facilitated, not by judgmentalism and disharmony, but by acceptance and unity.

### The conversation

Again this week we are imagining a conversation between Paul and two young Christians—Adelphos and Adelphe—who have come all the way from Rome to engage the apostle in a discussion of some of the things he wrote in his epistle to their church. Let's listen in:

**Adelphe:** Paul, of course you're right: obeying God's law, being the church of Jesus Christ...that's all about loving one another. But the reality back home in Rome is, we're trying to love one another, but we just can't seem to get past some of our differences. For instance, we're divided over worship days—we've got Sabbatarians and anti-Sabbatarians, disagreeing over which days to keep as holy. We've got food issues—on one side the Vegetarians, on the other the Carnivores, divided over groceries. What's a church to do?

*Paul: What a church must do, my good sister, is keep first things first. These are not insignificant issues, but neither are they primary issues. More important than days or groceries is the fellowship that our Lord died to redeem, and was raised to glorify. The weakest, pettiest, most annoying brother or sister you have in Rome is infinitely more important in the eyes of God than any day on the calendar or burger on the bun.*

*Whether a Christian is a Sabbatarian or an anti-Sabbatarian, he's part of the family of God; the day is important, but the worship is much more important. Whether a believer is a Vegetarian or a Carnivore, she's a member of the body of Christ. And don't ever forget, we are all guests at Christ's table.*

**Adelphe**: So…we should never do anything that might cause a brother to stumble, right? You said that in your letter to us, and I think I remember hearing you teach that here in Corinth (1 Cor 10:32).

*Paul: That's right. We should never disregard the conscience of a fellow Christian, especially if he's relatively young in the faith, and could be easily discouraged or confused by the actions of those of us who are more mature. But at the same time, weakness should not set the agenda. It would be foolish and disastrous to let weaker members of the body who, by virtue of their overly-scrupulous attitudes, control the church. No legalist (nor anyone else for that matter) should be allowed to highjack or paralyze the community of Christ just by saying, "That's a stumbling block for me!" Immature Christians need our tender patience and care, but they also need to grow up.*

**Adelphe**: So...how are we supposed to deal with these kinds of conflicts? Live with them? Ignore them? I mean, when you say *"Accept one another, just as Christ accepted you,"* just how far does that acceptance go? Is *any* behavior, any doctrinal position, "acceptable" within the church?

**Paul**: *That's a good question, one that has to be answered with a lot of wisdom and prayer. And, one that I suspect the church will continue to struggle with, even if the Lord doesn't come back for another 2000 years. Okay, let me organize my response to that good question around three principles:*

*First, we search for the truth in all things, but we differentiate between* primary *matters where we have a clear word from God, and* disputable *matters where we don't. Incarnation. Resurrection. Justification by grace. These are indispensable, central, crucial beliefs that undergird everything we know and teach about God and Christ.*

*Prayer. Communion. Baptism. These are vital connections to God and to the Cross; we could never consider them "unnecessary."*

*And certain commands from God—we talked about these last week—"Don't commit adultery." "Don't murder." "Don't steal." These are basic, non-negotiable values in our standard of living...and we can't "accept" a lower standard. Some beliefs and some behaviors are— if we're to use Scripture as our authority—simply "unacceptable."*

*Second, as we work these things out, we simply must extend grace to one another. That means, in this community, we give each other credit for the best motives. We sing one another's songs. And we give one another room to grow. We strive for maturity, but we never, ever condescend or adopt a judgmental spirit; that, my dear Adelphe is not "acceptable" either.*

*Jesus laid down his life for our forgiveness, not our judgmentalism...for our oneness, not our polarization. So whenever you find yourself slipping into an arrogant or judgmental mood about a brother, you need to say to yourself, "Christ died for him. Christ died...for him." In that last day when we have to give account for ourselves before the judgment seat of God—and we all will—God's not going to ask us to cite the Greek word for "baptize" or to spell "Melchizedek" (I hope)...but he is going to ask, "Did you love your brother?"*

*And third, we've got to learn, not just to live with but, to appreciate diversity in the body of Christ. We accept one another because God gave us to each other! That's why, as I wrote you, we need to make every effort humanly possible to do what makes for peace and mutual edification.*

**Adelphe**: Stop. Paul, I know I'm supposed to love all my brothers and sisters in church at Rome. I've got that. But I don't have to spend actual time with them, do I? I mean, I have absolutely nothing in common with some of those people. Some of them are slaves...some foreigners...some have the strangest ideas...and some are just older than dirt. Can't I just "love" them...from afar?

*Paul: Well, Adelphe, what did our Lord Jesus say? If you just keep company with people who look like you and dress like you and agree with every little word that comes out of your mouth, well then, big deal! What he actually said was, "If you only love those who love you back...if you only do good to those who do good to you...what credit is that to you? Everybody does that! You must love the unlovely, and be kind to the unkind, and give to people who have nothing to give back to you. You be merciful...like your Father God"* (Luke 6:32-36).

*How will we ever be the presence of Jesus Christ in this world if we don't take a risk and step outside our comfort zone with people? We belong to the Lord! What does it mean to be indwelt by the Holy Spirit, and saved by grace, if there is no fruit of the Spirit in our relationships, if we are not more gracious to people because we are Christ's than we would be on our own?*

*In the final analysis, Adelphe...grace is the answer, the answer to everything. What binds up the brokenhearted? Grace. What brings freedom to the oppressed? Grace. What inspires men and women to feed the hungry and show kindness to the stranger and clothe the naked and care for the suffering and visit the lonely? Grace. What brings estranged friends and estranged families and estranged nations back together? Grace. What holds diverse church families together? Grace. What is the heart of the gospel and the spirit of Christ and the hope of the world? Grace. Grace is the answer.*

*So let's not just say "grace" over meals. Let's do grace with one another. Let's extend grace to one another. Let's practice grace on one another. Let's live...GRACE. For this very reason, you know, Christ died and returned to life.*

### Growth's essential ingredient

Someone once asked Margaret Mead, the legendary anthropologist, "What's the earliest sign of civilization in an ancient society?" They expected her to say a clay pot, or a fish-hook, or a grinding stone. Instead her answer was, "A healed femur." The femur is the thigh-bone, the largest bone in the human body. And a *healed* femur means that while that person was injured, someone else cared for them—gathered food for them, tended to their injury, protected them in their vulnerability. You can't have civilization without compassion.

And you can't find your place of identity and service to God in this precarious world unless someone watches out for you now and then...unless someone accepts you during the "error" phase of trial-and-error...unless someone calls you to the highest standards of the Kingdom of God and forgives you when you fall short. As we are engaged in this primary spiritual business of "becoming ourselves" in God's world, there will be no ingredient more essential for the church to practice and to model than compassion, the very compassion of Christ.

Grace is the answer! Remember, the book of Romans was not written by Paul as a seminary textbook or an ecclesiastical rulebook, but as a letter *to* sinners *from* a sinner, a sinner whose only hope was the grace of God (Rom 3:23-24).

So here it is, then, the book of Romans in brief, "Romans for Dummies": 1—*We have all sinned and fallen short of the glory of God. 2—But we are justified freely by his grace. 3—Let us therefore present ourselves to him as a living sacrifice. 4—And let us in Christ accept one another, as Christ has accepted us.*

### Find a church

Please allow me one last word from our sponsor. As you begin the next chapter of your life out there in that precarious world, there is no task more important than this: *Find a church.*

Find a church that is compassionate, gracious, and relevant...and that is Christ-led, Spirit-energized, and Cross-centered.

Find a church that will engage all your conduits of worship every Sunday...and will send you out to live the living sacrifice between Sundays.

Find a church that will feed your peace...but will also feed your mind, and not permit you to be intellectually lazy.

Find a church that will allow you to think and question and doubt...but not allow you to become cynical.

Find a church that will nurture you in the primary spiritual task of "becoming yourself"...even as it challenges you to be conformed to the image and character of Christ himself.

Find a church that is a church of Jesus Christ...and become its most active and involved new member!

Your primary spiritual task is to become yourself. But you won't find yourself or become yourself...by yourself. For that you'll need a loving, accepting, challenging, God-hungry, Christ-centered, Spirit-empowered community around you. You'll need a church. *Find a church.*

Let's close with the wonderful benediction at the end of our text today, and let's make it our word of blessing for our graduates:

*May the God of hope fill you with all joy and peace as you trust in him,*

*so that you may overflow with hope by the power of the Holy Spirit.* (Rom 15:13)

## *Romans 16*
## *Introductory Comments*

Romans 16 is at first glance a pretty anti-climactic closing to a spectacular epistle, consisting mainly of 35 names of people we know little about. But this text's "liability" is its strength: it provides a very human portrait of Paul and his spiritual kinfolk, a first-century church directory (or prayer list) that fleshes out his sublime theology.

The function of this text is to remember and give thanks, and this sermon seeks to do the same: evoke listeners' memories of Christian friends and fellowship. Thus the objective of this sermon mirrors what James Thompson identifies as one of Paul's primary tasks in writing to the Romans: to bring heterogeneous groups together into one community—a "moral community"— reflecting God's image. I'm sure Paul's conspicuous mention of many indispensable Christian women in Rome evoked a bit of attention there, as it does here. Because names have faces, I made this sermon as visual as I knew how, using a delightful quote from a Fred Craddock sermon—one Stephen Farris also noted— which inspired the approach to this text. I closed the sermon with a series of eight illustrations, many of them visual, of lists of the names that put faces on "church."

The claim of the text: As these names of Paul's sisters and brothers trigger the names and faces of our own congregants, we are called again to the cross where Christ died, not for the whole world generically, but for each one of us by name.

# *Just Names*
## *Romans 16*

Today our series on Romans comes to a close. Every Sunday this spring we've tried to listen in on "the gospel according to Paul," his richest and most influential letter, written to a church whose Sunday services he had never attended.

Why did he write it? There's little evidence of any horrendous problems in Rome. It's not like Galatia, where *"another gospel"* was being preached and the church had lost its joy. It's nothing close to Corinth, where they were divided every conceivable way, and the Supper was a mess, and they weren't all that sure whether there had even been a resurrection. No, Paul has been pretty complimentary of the Roman believers:

> I myself am convinced, my brothers, that you yourselves are full of goodness, complete in knowledge and competent to instruct one another. I have written you quite boldly on some points, as if to remind you of them again, because of the grace God gave me to be a minister of Christ Jesus to the Gentiles with the priestly duty of proclaiming the gospel of God, so that the Gentiles might become an offering acceptable to God, sanctified by the Holy Spirit. (Rom 15:14-16)

So, why did he write? Clearly, Rome occupies an important place in Paul's thinking and planning as he looks to the future. He tells the Christians there that he has been longing for years to spend time with them on his way to Spain. I think Paul, like all good missionaries have had to do for the last 2000 years, is working on his "support." When he says in 15:24, *"I hope to...have you assist me"* (some translations say *"speed me on my journey"*), he may be talking about financial help from Rome, or even, setting up Rome as his new base of missionary operations. So perhaps in this letter we have Paul's doctrinal *vita*—certainly his *"gospel"* (a word he uses six times in the first seventeen verses)—laid out for the church in Rome: "Here's the message you'd be supporting."

### All these names?

It is kind of a shame, though, that as this series comes to an end, what we have to work with is just names. After fifteen chapters of thrilling words—*"justification," "reconciliation," "redemption"*...and beloved passages—*"No condemnation for those who are in Christ Jesus," "We are more than conquerors," "Nothing in all creation can separate us from the love of God"*...Romans closes with just a list of names. Thirty-five strange, hard-to-pronounce names, names such as *Epenetus, Ampliatus, Stachys* (What kind of mother names her boy Stachys?), *Asyncritus, Phlegon* (Phlegon? Sounds like a brand of dog collar).

And yet, you have to admit there's a lot of warmth and affection sprinkled amidst these names. Three times Paul calls someone *"dear friend"* (16:5, 9, 12). Another three times he refers to people as his *"relatives"* (16:7, 11, 21), which we take to mean, his fellow Jewish Christians. Ampliatus is described as one *"whom I love in the Lord"* (16:8). And Rufus' mother, Paul says, *"has been a mother to me"* (16:13).

I would not be a faithful handler of this text if I didn't point out something here that's truly unusual for an ancient letter or public document, and that's the inclusion of so many women's names. First and quite prominently, there's Phoebe, who apparently was the letter carrier who brought the letter of Romans to Rome. Paul describes her as a *"servant"* or *"deaconess"* (*diakonon*). Included as an "attachment" to one of the greatest theological works of all is what amounts to a letter of recommendation for Paul's good sister Phoebe. Is it possible that he sent Phoebe to Rome as his personal representative, to work out his support from the church there?

Then there's Priscilla, who's not only listed before her husband but, like Aquila, is called Paul's *"fellow-worker"* (or *"co-worker"*). Then Mary and Tryphena and Tryphosa and Persis and Rufus's mother and Julia and Nereus's sister. Three of the first five persons addressed, and at least eight in all, are women. In light of Paul's directions for some local churches to restrict some of the public activities of women in worship, it is interesting to note how he makes a point to highlight the names of many women in Rome who carry out significant roles of both service and leadership.

### The conversation

One last time we want to eavesdrop on an imaginary conversation between Paul and a brother and sister who have traveled far from their hometown of Rome to cross-examine the man who wrote an extraordinary letter to their church.

**Adelphos**: Well, Paul, my sister Adelphe and I have been here in Corinth with you for—what's it been?— fifteen weeks now. We've enjoyed the fellowship of all the

Christians here. We've certainly been made to feel welcome by your host Gaius, who has opened his home to us, just as he does every Lord's Day to the entire assembly. But most of all, Paul, we've been blessed by your willingness to let us wrestle together with the will and the Word of God.

*Paul: Ah, the blessing has been all mine, Adelphos. You know, don't you, what the great name "Israel" means? It means, "He wrestles…he struggles…with God." I would wish that all young Christians could be as straightforward and as open as you've been with me, in their search for deeper faith and understanding of God. God and his truth are never threatened by sincere questioning. Honest doubt is more the friend of truth than mindless assent, if…it keeps on—as our Lord dared us to do—"asking, seeking, and knocking."*

**Adelphe**: We fully intend to do that, Paul. And don't worry — by the time you visit us in Rome, Adelphos and I will have a whole new list of questions for you!

*Paul: Somehow I thought you would.*

**Adlephe**: Okay, but before we go, we wanted to ask you, Paul, what can we do for you? I know we're still pretty new in the faith, but is there anything a couple of young Christians can do for a veteran minister like you?

*Paul: That's a generous offer, Adelphe. And yes, there is: you can pray for me. Hand in hand or thousands of miles apart, that's something powerful we Christians can always do for one another. Pray strenuously for me, that my ministry may not be derailed by my opponents. (I've had some pretty close calls already, and some of my enemies in Judea are especially scary.) Pray that I can continue to bring aid to the poor. Pray that I might get to carry the good news all the way to Spain. And of course, pray that I might make it one day soon to your great city of Rome and receive the refreshment of being with your church family.*

**Adelphos**:  That we can do, and will, gladly. But speaking of our church family…my goodness, Paul, judging from your epistle to us…you know more people in our home church than we do! Who are all those names you mention at the very end?

*Paul:  You don't know all those names? Well, since we've grown close these last few months, and since you're leaving town tomorrow, let me be as candid with you as you've been with me. (I wrote to you boldly; I'll speak to you the same way.) Adelphos, it's your business to find out who those names belong to! Is it possible that you guys might have been spending a little too much time with just the part of the body that's most like you?*

*Take Phoebe, for instance. When I sent her to Rome, carrying my epistle to you all, I sent you one of the finest servants in our fellowship. I wanted her to bring to your fellowship the same spiritual leadership that she demonstrated in Cenchrea, near here. You have a lot to learn from sisters like Phoebe. There's Epenetus: find him and ask him what it's like to be the very first person in your corner of the world to say, "Yes, I'll be baptized into Christ." Andronicus and Junias—we did jail time together; ask them about the cost of discipleship. Or here's an idea: go spend a day with women like Tryphena and Tryphosa and Persis, and if you can keep up with them, see what you'll learn about being industrious Christian workers just for the joy of it. What you need to do when you get home, my children, is get out the old church directory and start networking!*

**Adelphe**:  Thanks for being candid, Paul (as if you've ever been otherwise). Sounds like there are quite a few mentors in the faith back home that we need to take advantage of. So…as our conversation comes to a close…any parting thoughts?

*Paul: Well, since you asked…I believe I'll do a little review. (Forgive me, but old Gamaliel drummed it into our heads that any rabbi worth his salt always makes sure his students at least get the basics.) If you didn't hear anything else I said in my letter, hear this, loud and clear:*

*One, we are sinners, every one of us; we're not "dysfunctional"; we're not "error-prone"; we're not practitioners of "alternative lifestyles"; we're sinners, and that's the truth of it. Two,—don't ask me why because I don't know why—God loves us anyway, gratuitously, loved us to the extent that he would give up Jesus, his beloved, to be our sin-bearer, that by grace we might be justified, reconciled, saved!…if we take hold of that grace in obedient faith. Three, as the atonement was costly, so is the obedience: it calls for nothing less than the placing of ourselves—body and soul—on the altar of God as living sacrifices, that we might daily die to ego and greed and hate and bigotry and everything else that got us into our sorry sinful state in the first place. And four, now that we find ourselves in the family of God, we simply must learn to love…one…another.*

*We have to love one another enough to protect and maintain the unity of the Spirit in the body of Christ. That means we don't allow divisive, immature people to compromise our oneness. We don't allow little elitist groups to form in the church. We don't let people spread foolish, self-indulgent ideas just because they have sophisticated vocabularies. In a world where evil is so intelligent, the last thing we followers of Christ can afford to be, is naïve…so we have to be very smart about being "fools for Christ!" If I were your commencement speaker, my advice would be: "Graduate summa cum laude in the ways of goodness, and fail miserably in the curriculum of evil." Or as our Lord put it, "Be as shrewd as snakes and as innocent as doves" (Matt 10:16).*

*So when you get home to Rome…I hope you'll want to go back to your house church there in Priscilla and Aquila's home, and commit yourselves to a deeper understanding of these primary Christian concepts and doctrines that we've been discussing together. But I hope it will be just as high a priority for you to commit yourselves to a deeper understanding of your brothers and sisters there. You see…gospel of Jesus Christ—it's about atonement AND it's about Ampliatus…it's about faith AND it's about Phoebe…do you get my point? The gospel is about propositions AND it's about people. As I've been telling the church here in Corinth, you can speak in tongues, and you can speak in prophecies, but if you're not speaking in love, then you are just so much religious noise (1 Cor 13:1-3). Put another way, your doctrine is not sound, if it's just a lot of sound. "By this," he said, "by THIS…shall the world know that you are mine…if you love one another" (John 13:35).*

*So my dear children, as we part company for a time, I charge you to be faithful. Keep on asking, seeking, and knocking. Keep the church loving one another (keep that wonderful exchange of the holy kiss going every Sunday). And keep in mind that you are part of a great international church family. So when you stand up in the assembly in a few weeks and make your report on our conversations…please pass on to your sisters and brothers not only my love and best wishes, but also those of all the churches of Christ all over this world. Tell them, "The churches of Christ salute you!"*

*Now, go with God. I pray you grace. And I wish you peace. To the only wise God be glory forever, through Christ Jesus! Amen.*

### Fleshing out the names

Isn't it a shame the great book of Romans closes on such an anti-climactic note? Not with a bang but a whimper. Just a bunch of names.

Dr. Fred Craddock, in a sermon he called, *"When the Roll is Called Down There,"* does a pretty good job fleshing out the names:

> There's Mary. Mary worked hard. She was there when everybody else quit. She's the one who always said, 'Now, Paul, you go on home; I'll put things up. I'll put the hymnals away, and I'll pick up all the papers and straighten the chairs. You go on home; you're tired.' 'Well, Mary, you're tired, too.' 'Yes, Paul, but you've got to ride a donkey across Asia tomorrow. You go on. I'll pick up here.' Mary worked hard.
>
> Epaenetus, the first person converted under my preaching, and I didn't sleep a wink that night saying, 'Thank God. Finally somebody heard.' The first one to respond to the gospel. What a marvelous day that was! Tryphaena and Tryphosa, obviously twins. You hear it, don't you, in the names? Tryphaena and Tryphosa. They always sat on this side, and they both wore blue every Sunday. I never knew them apart, really. One of them had a mole on her cheek, but I didn't know if it was Tryphaena or Tryphosa. I never did get them straight…

You know one thing I think Paul could be doing by calling all these names? He may be making sure <u>his</u> name is on some prayer lists!

> I urge you, brothers, by our Lord Jesus Christ and by the love of the Spirit, to join me in my struggle by praying to God for me. Pray that I may be rescued from the unbelievers in Judea and that my service in Jerusalem may be acceptable to the saints there, so that by God's will I may come to you with joy and together with you be refreshed. (Rom 15:30-32)

He calls their names, in hopes they'll call his, before the throne of grace.

A few weeks ago I passed among you a copy of "Schindler's List." All it is, is just names, 1132 names pecked out on an old German typewriter. And yet…every name on that list meant salvation, liberation, life.

My favorite monument in Washington, D.C., is the Lincoln Memorial. What a magnificent statue. What a magnificent setting. Sometimes when I visited Mr. Lincoln, if I had a little extra time I would wander over to another monument nearby. Quite a contrast to the Lincoln Memorial. It's a wall, just a long, black wall…full of names. No great words from the Gettysburg Address or the Second Inaugural. Just names. But every time I visited the Wall I looked for and located the one name I know on it: *John Grimenstein*, my good friend who went to Vietnam and never came home.

Then there was the day in Springfield, Missouri, on the campus of Southwest Missouri State University, when I walked through a gymnasium in which every available inch was covered with home-made quilts. But it wasn't a crafts fair. Every quilt bore a name, the name of someone who had died of AIDS. A woman was reading off the names at a microphone, but she broke down and had to be replaced by someone else. Apparently she knew someone on that list of names.

I have here today a framed professional photograph, entitled, "Raven's Run, Kentucky." It was given me by the Southside Church of Christ campus ministry group when we moved away in 1980. On the back of the photo—completely spoiling its resale value—are all these people's names. Every name sparks a memory. (Except *Jacques*—I don't have a clue who *Jacques* is.) *Ron*—I did his and *Jackie's* wedding...and here's the couple who sweetly drove me crazy...and there's *Tom* and *Jan*, who woke me up at 1:00 in the morning wanting to be baptized...and *Stan* and *Donna*, who became medical missionaries in South America.

Here's a photo (not professional at all) of the Spanish-speaking members of the Church of Christ in Falls Church. And the Spanish Bible, the *Santa Biblia*, they also gave me when we moved here from Virginia. And inside the front cover—you guessed it—they all wrote their names. Spanish names: *Esteban, Idalia, Luis, Maria*. Here's my brother *Roberto*, from Guatemala, who makes the hottest chili in the Western World. I'll never forget the summer day we stood in a stifling hot auditorium and heard him take the oath as an American citizen. And his dear wife *Blanca*; she lost a daughter who was a freedom-fighter in Nicaragua. So many names.

Some of you will recognize this: it's the program from last Friday's Pepperdine graduation exercises. We sat there on that uncharacteristically blustery day and listened while Don Thompson read out over 550 names! Another name, and another name...Because we had good seats near the photographers who captured each new grad as he or she came off the stage, I got to watch as each name turned into a face and each face burst into a huge smile. But it was name number 146 I was there to hear and to cheer: *Jennifer Anne Durham.*

And here's a list of names: *Archer, Atkinson, Atkisson, Azadian, Bachelor, Backowski, Baird.* It's the phone directory of the Malibu Church of Christ. Just a five-page printout of some names. Big deal. "What's in a name? A rose by any other name would smell as sweet," right? But what this is, this bunch of names, is a CHURCH. This is what Jesus came to earth to build. A fellowship. A family. A redeemed, sanctified, commissioned list of names.

That is why Jesus came. And that is why Jesus died. For these names. Our names. And that—I suspect—is why Paul ends the book of Romans with...just a list of names.